Everybody Loves Polar Bears

A Polar Paired Romantic Comedy

LoLo Paige

Published by Avoca Press Publishing, 2023.

To Marc, the love of my life

Who taught me the importance of a keystone species in an ecosystem.

Everybody Loves Polar Bears
The Polar Paired Romantic Comedy Series
Copyright © 2023 by LoLo Paige
ISBN: 978-1-7360951-4-0
First published by Avoca Press Publishing 2023

All rights reserved. No part of this publication may be reproduced, stored, or transmitted in any form or by any means, electronic, mechanical, photocopying, recording, scanning, or otherwise, without written permission from the publisher. It is illegal to copy this book, post it to a website, or distribute it by any other means without permission.

This is a work of fiction. Though based on events in actual settings, it is an imaginary story. The author has taken artistic license with details regarding locations and activities for the story to flow smoothly. Any resemblance to actual persons, living or dead, is entirely coincidental. The publisher and the book are not associated with any product, real person, or vendor mentioned in this book. None of the companies referenced within the book have endorsed the book.

Cover Design by M. Culler
Edited by Judy McCrary, Evil Commas.com

Chapter 1

"Stop! Don't shoot!" Macy Applegate held her arm out in a stop motion as her pulse raced. The urgency in her words caused every head in the room to swivel in her direction.

"Polar bears deserve to exist the same as humans do. I won't let you shoot them!" Macy poured her heart and soul into every word.

"Get out of my way, or I'll shoot *you*," growled the man in a menacing tone.

She lifted her chin and studied him. Her mind blanked when she locked onto the glacial stare of the fair-haired man firmly planted in front of her.

"Um... where did I leave off?" She frantically searched for her line, clutching the pages with trembling fingers.

"I'll have to shoot you," he said impatiently, waving his folded script.

"I sure hope not." Macy raised her eyes to find him watching her. She fought to control her nerves and let out an impatient sigh. "May I please start again? I lost my concentration." Heat radiated her cheeks as she chastised herself for her lack of professionalism.

"No," he said tersely. "Continue." He glanced at his wristwatch, then crossed his arms as if he had something better to do.

Nick Westwood had introduced himself as the assistant director for this movie. Before her audition, she'd looked up the production staff online. Westwood had earned a stellar reputation in the film industry—probably why he was so snooty.

He offered her an expectant, disgruntled look. "Well? I'm not getting any younger here."

She sucked in a deep breath so as not to call him a smartass. Instead, she focused on her sides from the script. "Don't want to shoot you," she read, punching each word while she meant the opposite.

"Wrong line. Yours is the one *after* that." His condescension gave her the impression he thought her to be one click short of being an idiot.

Normally, she was calm and composed during an audition, but her nerves jangled whenever she glanced at this guy with his beauty-school-dropout tousled hair. She figured he deliberately styled it to mimic a windswept look, like he'd just blown in from trekking a nearby glacier.

"Sorry. I knew that." Her cheeks heated as she put her finger on the next line, afraid she'd mess it up. "I'm determined to save these polar bears. If I must, I'll take a bullet for them—" She stopped and grimaced.

Westwood's mosaics of blue ice locked her in a stony stare. "Why'd you stop? Keep going." He darted another glance at his wristwatch.

I must be taking up too much time, she chided herself.

Macy leaned in to examine the script, and in the name of taking up even more time, she pointed something out. "Hate to toss a monkey wrench into this, but does it really make sense for this character to say she'd take a bullet for a polar bear? It sounds like dialogue from a cheesy 'B' movie. But who am I to judge? I'm not a screenwriter," she added sweetly.

EVERYBODY LOVES POLAR BEARS

Westwood cocked a brow. "*Everybody Loves Polar Bears* is a movie about saving polar bears from extinction," he said with an air of condescension.

"My understanding is this movie is also about conserving arctic marine life and preventing population declines of keystone species in a climate change environment. Polar bears being one of those keystone species," she said with an air of authority.

"That's what I said in a nutshell." Curiosity wrinkled his face. "And you know this because?"

"I study this subject in my line of work. It's right there on my resume." She pointed.

He glanced down at a clipboard on the small table next to him. "I see, but you aren't here to evaluate the script. Please read what's there. Cripes, everyone's a critic," he muttered, giving her a hard look. "And let's see some emotion this time."

I'll bet he practices that crabby expression in the mirror to unnerve people. You want emotion? I'll give you some emotion, buddy.

Resolute, Macy cleared her throat, eyeballing the camera on its tripod, the blinking red light reminding her it was recording. She pictured Westwood aiming an AR-15 on a blinky-eyed polar bear so she'd have motivation to narrow her gaze into a killer stink-eye.

"If you shoot these bears, I guarantee it'll be the *last* thing you ever shoot!" she growled, punching every word. She almost said 'punk' like Harry Callahan in the 1970s *Dirty Harry* movie, but it was a tad outdated.

Westwood flinched and cocked a brow. "That's not what the script says."

"I tweaked it to be more plausible. Don't you think?" Macy beamed at him.

"I believe we're done here. Thanks for coming in," he said in a clipped manner.

Her proud smile dribbled to the floor. "But I'm not finished! Let me start over—I'm a local stage actress—I have excellent reviews with lead roles. Like I said, it's all on my resume—"

He cut in. "I understand, but we've heard enough. Thank you." He nudged the man sitting beside him, tapping maniacally on his phone. "Josh, get her headshot before she goes."

The dark-haired man raised his phone. He smirked, ogling her with a lingering once-over. "Smile, beautiful."

She tried forcing her mouth upward, but all she could summon was a stunned, pissed-off expression. If they needed a disgruntled extra, she could totally play that part. In spades.

The other guy tapped his phone to photograph her, then went back to splitting atoms or whatever the heck else he was doing.

"But... I'd like to finish this scene," she pleaded. "I spent the entire weekend preparing for this audition. I can do this. I'm just nervous."

"Everyone is nervous when they audition." Westwood flashed her a stiff but pearly smile.

Macy was no stranger to auditioning—she knew the sting of obvious rejection but stayed composed out of principle. She regarded Nick Westwood with an unblinking stare. Despite her twisted insides, she steeled herself.

"You didn't like my audition, did you?" she challenged.

Westwood picked up the clipboard with her audition sheet. "You did fine."

"But not good enough, right? Let me do it again. Give me a chance, please..." Begging wasn't her style, but she wanted this badly. She tried to gauge Westwood's expression behind his cool mask of indifference but could only guess what he was thinking, since his glacial stare matched his frosty demeanor.

"Trust me, you did great," he repeated, his voice devoid of expression, as he scribbled on her audition sheet.

I know where this is heading. Nowhere.

Macy sized the guy up. Hollywood handsome and then some, a few crow's feet from squinting in the L.A. sunshine. She guessed him to be thirty-five, maybe forty if he did Botox, which he probably did. They all did. The muscular arms and broad shoulders told her he was no stranger to a gym.

"Miss Applegate?"

She snapped out of her jaded assessment. "Yes?"

"We'll be in touch, to let you know."

"Thank you," Macy forced out. The words stuck like toads in her throat. She didn't stand a snowball's chance of getting cast in this movie.

Macy pictured Westwood next to his outdoor pool at his palatial digs up on Mulholland Drive, tall palms waving, the Hollywood Hills framing him while he barked into his phone with a studio executive—his bathrobe strategically hung open so his household staff could swoon over his gym-centric body.

"Thanks for coming in." Westwood's finger brushed hers as she handed him the script pages. She caught the scent of a great-smelling cologne, reeking of Rodeo Drive.

His eyes swept over her like an icy wave, and for a millisecond she thought she detected a smidgeon of amiability. But then, this guy couldn't be friendly if his life depended on it.

"I look forward to hearing from you," she said authoritatively, as if she were the one casting this movie. As she put on her bright-colored Alaskan parka, she noticed Westwood eyeballing it.

"This isn't real fur," she rushed to explain, fingering the arctic fox fur ruff around the hood and cuffs. It was indeed real, but she didn't want the Hollywood contingent regarding Alaskans as animal-trapping savages. Then again, why should she care?

Because I want a part in this movie.

Macy berated herself for her last-ditch suck-up effort to get cast.

"I wasn't judging," Westwood tossed out lamely. His baseball cap sported a fighting salmon with a lure in its mouth.

Aww, how quaint: Hollywood guy wants to fit in with the locals.

"When can I expect to hear from you?" she asked as she removed her heels and bent to tug on her *Xtratufs* snow boots.

He stood with folded arms, studying her. "Someone will be in touch."

She waited for the when, but he didn't give her one. Instead, his words hung in the air between them like a suspension bridge over a rushing glacial river.

So much for this audition.

"Well, thank you. Good luck with your production." Macy picked up her purse from a nearby chair and turned to go.

"Miss Applegate?" Westwood called after her. "What's your reason for auditioning for *Everybody Loves Polar Bears?*"

She twisted around in surprise and stared at him like he'd sprouted fairy wings.

Isn't it obvious? Is this guy for real?

"Everyone has a reason. What do you hope to get out of this if we cast you?" He looked at her expectantly.

"All right." She thought for a moment. "Polar bears are at the top of the food chain and play a vital role in the overall health of the Arctic marine environment. This movie will raise awareness of the plight of this species that is heading toward extinction. Without polar bears, the food chain would be severely disrupted..." she trailed off, catching his amused stare.

"You sound like an environmental impact statement." He folded his arms and smirked, as if he'd heard this reasoning countless times. "Now, tell me the real reason."

"That *is* the real reason," she bristled, unappreciative of his deprecating attitude.

What the heck would Mr. Congeniality know about environmental impact statements? That was *her* line of work.

"Everyone wants to save the polar bears. Now, instead of narrating a National Geo documentary, how about you tell me why you're here?" The intensity of his stare ruffled her stomach.

Macy swallowed and lifted her chin. "In that case, if you must know. I want an acting career. A real one, where I make a living. I have enough acting experience. I believe I have something to offer." Her words came out more defiant than she'd intended, but there it was... her God's honest truth.

Westwood raised his brows. "Now *that* I believe."

"Okay then. Thank you for the opportunity to audition." She punctuated it with a quick zip of her parka, grabbed her oversized purse, and headed for the door.

"Thanks for coming in," he said evenly with a quick nod.

Disappointment burned through Macy as she hurried down the carpeted hallway of the midtown Anchorage office building. She exited onto the sidewalk leading to the parking lot on Northern Lights Boulevard, where ten-degree air assaulted her senses—a reminder that January was ready to hand off its torch of subarctic chill to February. She stepped across the patchy ice to her car.

A nosy raven perched atop a light pole sent cheerful, musical clicks down to her as if to say, "Don't worry, honey, you've got this." He followed up with a gurgling croak.

Macy looked up warily. "Thanks, Mr. Nevermore. Please don't drop a gift on my windshield." Raven turds on a windshield at ten degrees had a way of hardening like petrified wood.

She berated herself for her botched audition. Though the Westwood guy had been terse, Macy knew better than to burn bridges. She'd wanted a role in this movie, ever since the announcement on local news. Film acting classes had filled her schedule outside of work, and she'd practiced reading lines with any warm body she could find. She'd even practiced lines while driving around town.

She figured it would have been easier to start her career in Alaska before pursuing opportunities in Los Angeles. Down there, she'd be another in a long line of aspiring actors, working odd jobs and waiting for a breakout role. In the meantime, she'd likely be waiting tables, cleaning toilets, or vacuuming heaven knows what from a porn actor's pool.

In Alaska, she could have distinguished herself. But her hopes went up in flames with her botched audition for Mr. Congeniality. Macy thought of Westwood's no-nonsense expression. She'd grown accustomed to working in a mostly male environment in her federal agency and was used to dealing with the occasional grumpy sunshine, but this guy didn't even give her a chance.

And there wasn't any hint of sunshine. Not even grumpy sunshine.

More like a cranky polar bear... with attitude.

Chapter 2

Macy had clicked the remote start on her key fob from inside the building, so her car would warm up by the time she got inside. Up here, north of sixty degrees latitude, Alaskans considered remote starts more of a necessity than a luxury. It wasn't uncommon to see empty idling vehicles in parking lots around Anchorage in January, clouds of exhaust billowing in the frosty air.

Just as she reached her car, a large blue van pulled up and out clambered human-sized animals—a tuxedoed puffin, a furry moose, and a polar bear.

"Hey, George! What are you doing here?" Macy greeted the puffin with a wave.

It had become routine for her to see animal rights activists at public meetings, holding up signs and chanting. They mostly showed up for proposed energy projects in Alaska, but it surprised her to see them outside of the film office.

"What's up, Macy? Fancy seeing you here," responded a friendly male voice from inside the round furry puffin. He lifted a black wing in greeting, his black and white torso and humongous orange feet a comical contrast to the stark wintry conditions.

Macy always thought puffins looked like birds wearing fancy tuxes.

"Are you protesting the polar bear movie?" Macy was on a congenial first name basis with the puffin and the moose. However, she had a history of contentious encounters with Meadow, the polar bear, during public meetings with her agency.

"Yes, we are!" The moose lifted a furry hoof in a wave.

"Why? It's about saving polar bears," Macy pointed out, mystified.

The moose turned, and one of her furry antlers smacked the polar bear in the snout.

"Hey, watch it, Alice!" shouted the polar bear, stumbling back.

Macy suppressed a laugh. The oversized animals reminded her of cartoons in the herky-jerky way they clomped around.

The polar bear spoke up. "We want to make sure the filming is humane and compliant with wildlife protection laws. And that all live animals in this movie are treated with the respect they deserve." The nasally female voice emanating from the bear was not one of Macy's favorite people.

"Hello, Meadow." Macy addressed the furry white bear, expecting to lock horns with her for the zillionth time.

Meadow lifted a "Treat Polar Bears With Respect!" sign on a stick high above her white furry head.

The puffin, aka George, waddled over to Macy. "We called Channel 2 news, so they'd cover our activity here today."

"Of course you did." Macy rolled her eyes and opened the driver's side door to her idling vehicle. "I'm sure the movie people will appreciate the publicity. See you all on the evening news."

The puffin and the moose waved goodbye. "See you in the next dogfight, Macy!"

"I can't wait." Macy shot them a fake grin and sank into the driver's seat. She shifted her medium-sized SUV into reverse just as a lengthy black limo pulled up and stopped behind her car, blocking her from backing out.

EVERYBODY LOVES POLAR BEARS

Macy slammed her brakes. "Dammit!"

She was about to lean on the horn when Nick Westwood appeared from the building and smacked straight into the puffin. George the puffin fought for balance as he and Westwood stumbled back. The puffin windmilled his wings to save himself from splatting onto the icy pavement. He lost the battle and went down for the count, flat on his back.

"Oh, no!" Macy clambered from the driver's seat and hurried toward the prone puffin. "George, are you okay?"

He whimpered as he lay motionless, like a slug.

Westwood took hold of a stubby wing to help the puffin regain his feet as the moose and polar bear advanced on him.

"You should be ashamed of yourself for picking on a poor, defenseless puffin!" bellowed the moose as George grappled with his orange, colossal feet. They reminded Macy of seaplane pontoons made of pumpkins.

"Hey, Mr. Hollywood, that's animal cruelty! We don't put up with that here!" growled the polar bear, lifting a massive faux fur paw to take a swing at Westwood.

"Back off! I didn't shove him!" shouted Westwood, as he blocked the paw with one hand. His other hand balled into a fist, and he punched the bear in the snout.

Meadow's nose crumpled as her polar bear snout morphed into a Pekinese. She staggered back into the moose. They both went down like dominoes, grunting and sprawling on the snow-covered concrete.

Macy clamped a gloved hand over her nose and mouth. Now there were three over-sized animals down on a midtown Anchorage sidewalk during rush hour. Anyone passing by might think it was hunting season. And as luck would have it, the

Channel 2 news van pulled up in time to see the casualties splayed on the pavement.

"Oh, that's freaking dandy!" Westwood backed up with a baffled expression. "What the hell is this? We aren't the government or the oil industry. Why are they protesting *us?*" he asked Macy as if she were supposed to know the answers. He lifted his arms and dropped them in a bewildered manner.

"Because you're Hollywood." Macy glanced at poor old Puffin George, who was still having trouble getting his ginormous feet under him to stand up.

"I'm not the bad guy here," mumbled Westwood, squaring his shoulders.

The dark-haired reporter scurried over, while her assistant pointed his TV camera at the animals rolling around on the sidewalk. "What happened here?"

The camera swung toward Macy and Westwood as she tugged the puffin to his feet. Westwood helped the moose stand on her hind hooves, while the polar bear cussed a blue streak.

"He punched me! That's aggravated assault on a polar bear. I'm filing charges!" Meadow cried out from under her crumpled bear nose.

Westwood attempted to fix it, but Meadow batted his hand away with a humongous paw. "Don't touch me, you savage!"

As the camera guy closed in on Westwood and the misshapen polar bear, Macy bit her lip to keep a straight face at the smashed-in snout of the beleaguered polar bear, alongside Westwood's wild-eyed look.

His hand shot out to push the camera back. "Shut off the damn camera." He stared at the reporter. "Please!" Westwood growled, as Macy helped the polar bear to her feet.

EVERYBODY LOVES POLAR BEARS

The news crew ignored his pleas.

On impulse, Macy intervened. "Hi, Amber. Can you please not record this?" She knew the reporter from past interviews as part of her day job. "This isn't good publicity for the company planning to film a movie that adds to our Anchorage economy. They could easily leave and film it down in Vancouver. Then Alaska would lose out. I shouldn't have to explain."

Westwood shot her a startled look while the pretty reporter considered. "Turn off the camera," she instructed her coworker.

"Thank you," said Macy. "This doesn't need to be on tonight's news. Instead, do a feel-good story about this movie being filmed in Anchorage."

"Hey, turn that camera back on! This guy busted my nose. *And he hit a woman!*" sputtered Meadow's muffled voice from inside the white distorted head. She aimed her paw at Westwood. "You're on the hook for a new polar bear suit, Hollywood."

"Sorry, I didn't know you were a woman. Not that I'd hit a man either—and I didn't hit *you*—I hit the damn bear! Besides, you swung at me first."

"You shoved George and made him fall!" the polar bear countered. "He probably hit his head and has a concussion, isn't that right, George?"

Puffin George mumbled something unintelligible as he teetered on his massive pumpkin feet.

"Are you okay, bro?" Westwood peered into the puffin's eyeholes.

"Yeah, pretty much," replied the puffin, trying to brush snow from his white tuxedoed belly with his stubby wing.

"It's your fault George fell," persisted the polar bear.

"I didn't push him!" Westwood shot back. "When I came outside, the puffin was in my way, and I accidentally bumped into him." Westwood appeared agitated as he marched up to the limousine behind Macy's Highlander. "Send me the bill. I'll replace your animal suit!" he called over his shoulder.

The reporter barraged Macy with questions. "Did you see the movie director deliberately shove these animals?"

"No, I saw him bump into the puffin just as he said. The polar bear swung at him first. And he isn't the director, he's the—" Macy stopped. She wasn't altogether sure what Westwood was. The production credited him as the assistant director, but he also appeared to be the casting director. The movie world was confusing.

"Not true!" shouted the polar bear. "You saw him shove me first, then he punched me, and you know it!"

"I know what I saw." A sudden thought struck Macy—if she defended Westwood, she'd be perceived as taking his side, and if she stuck up for the animal rights activists, she'd be viewed as taking theirs. The day job with her federal agency was to remain neutral, and although it had nothing to do with this film, she didn't want her worlds colliding.

"Says here Westwood is the assistant director for this production," said the reporter, swiping her finger on her digital tablet.

"I wouldn't know about that," shrugged Macy. "Look, I have to be somewhere." She wanted out of this situation, but the limo still blocked her car.

Lovely.

She stepped to her car and swung open the door. "Excuse me, I need to get out. Please tell the driver to move," she hollered at

EVERYBODY LOVES POLAR BEARS

Westwood, who stood yammering into an open window of the limo.

"No, Dylan! No more rewrites." Westwood appeared agitated. "We have a tight schedule and don't have time for this. You'll deliver the lines as written."

Dylan Ford must be inside the limo!

Macy craned her neck to glimpse America's hottest movie star, but Westwood blocked her view. The dark-tinted window slid up, and the never-ending vehicle sped off, leaving him in a cloud of frosty exhaust.

Westwood turned and marched toward the building. To avoid bumping into her, he stopped in his tracks, glancing at the local news team conversing with the costumed animals in front of the building entrance. He leaned toward Macy, his breath puffing out in fast, frosty clouds.

"Thanks for helping me out back there. I appreciate it." He dipped a nod before striding into the building, disregarding shouts from the TV reporter and rants from the moose and polar bear. The puffin hollered thanks for helping him up.

Macy quietly slipped into her car before the reporter could rush up and shove a mic in her face. She backed out of the parking space and headed home. She turned onto the snow-covered driveway to her condo, cut the engine, and hurried inside to turn on the local news. Tonight's slant should prove interesting. She was curious to see how the reporter would depict the good-looking assistant movie director.

Probably not in a good light. But what did she care? Westwood's condescending attitude during her audition left a lasting impression, and while he'd thanked her, she couldn't help but think of him as an arrogant jerk.

Maybe he'd cut her some slack and consider casting her in the movie as a token of gratitude? All she needed was a foot in the door.

Yeah, fat chance. Like that'll happen.

Chapter 3

Nick Westwood stood from the conference table in the downtown film office to pour himself another cup of coffee. One thing about being back in Alaska, the coffee was outstanding. He savored the flavor of his favorite blend of Thunderclap coffee.

"We need to get this cast list completed," said the movie's director, Logan DeMello, shuffling papers at one end of the table. "Part of the film permit agreement with the state was to cast as many Alaskans as possible."

Nick returned to his seat. "Hundreds showed up at auditions. Couldn't believe the turnout after spreading the word on local news channels and social media."

"What about this beauty?" Josh, the casting director in name only—according to Nick—slid an audition sheet across the table with a picture of Macy Applegate. Her auburn hair and smoldering green eyes stared out at them, her 'don't screw with me' expression radiating off the paper.

Nick recalled Miss Applegate's audition and her remark about the cringe-worthy dialogue. He'd agreed it was cheesy and made a mental note to run it by DeMello, but that wasn't the sort of thing you admitted to someone in an audition.

He slid the sheet back to Josh and raised a brow. "This one might be pretty, but she could prove difficult to work with. Remember the tough time she gave me at the audition? Oh, that's right." He paused for effect. "You were busy making love to your phone."

Josh ignored Nick's jibe, looking everywhere but in his direction.

"Why'd she give you a hard time?" DeMello asked Nick, rubbing a hand over his short, gray hair. "Usually, it's the other way around."

"I didn't let her finish the reading. We were running behind," replied Nick. "I was tired and out of patience."

"I keep telling you to work on your people skills." DeMello flicked his eyes at Nick. "Can she at least act? What age group is she in?"

"She can act. Good facial expression." Nick peered at her audition sheet. "Says here she's thirty-five. She was none too happy when I didn't let her finish reading. We were running low on time, so I said we'd let her know."

DeMello adjusted his reading glasses and tilted his head to evaluate. "Then cast her as an extra. We can use another thirty-something. What do you think, Josh?" He gave the audition sheet to the dark-haired casting director.

"Hot. Foxy redhead. I would do her in a heartbeat," smirked Josh, practically drooling on the photo.

Nick shot an intense glare in Josh's direction. "You won't be doing her or anyone else during this production. Especially local talent. Not here. Not in this town."

"Chill, Westwood." Josh leaned back in his chair with a derisive grin. "You need to get hold of that temper."

"And you need to dial back your lazy attitude. How about you do your job, so I don't have to do it?" Nick wasn't in the mood to cover for another coddled twenty-something son of a famous film executive. "Don't even think about bedding down the locals we hire for this movie. Got that?" His words echoed around the room like acid rain splashing on a pristine pond.

"You can't tell me what I can and can't do in my off time, old man," needled Josh.

Nick glanced at DeMello. "Step in anytime, Logan. You're the head honcho." He was tired of playing the heavy in every production. The movie director avoided confrontation like covid, so the nepotism snowflakes got away with not doing their damn jobs. Everyone else kissed the venerated ass of this executive producer's snot-nosed kid, but Nick refused to do it. And he seethed from the sting of the 'old man' comment.

"Enough, you two. I need you to be civil," admonished DeMello. "You don't have to be chummy. Just work together." He turned to Josh. "Nick is the assistant director on this production, and my right hand. What he says goes."

"Yeah, about that. My father said you'd guarantee me the first A.D. position," whined Josh, glancing at Nick with annoyance. "Why is he the A.D. instead of me?"

DeMello cleared his throat. "You really want me to answer that?" His middle-aged demeanor reminded Nick of a high school discipline principal.

Nick chuckled and grabbed a stack of audition sheets. He tossed Macy Applegate's at Josh. "Make yourself useful. Tack this onto the hired extras board." He wasn't sure if he'd regret hiring Macy Applegate. She would be challenging to work with, but he appreciated how she'd helped him out during the protest debacle.

"Oh, yeah, I have a note about some of the dialogue," said Nick offhandedly.

"What about it?" DeMello popped a stick of gum in his mouth and offered Nick one. He declined.

"There's a line about taking a bullet for a polar bear. Sounds cheesy. This isn't a secret service spy thriller."

"Seriously? That's a line in the script? I agree. Strike it." DeMello waved his hand. "Make sure the script supervisor gets the note."

"Yep. Will do." Nick made another mental note to tell Macy Applegate he took her suggestion to heart once she was onboard. Although the vibe he'd gotten from her wasn't a friendly one. No, it was more of a determined one.

He thought back to when he'd first started out in the movie world. He'd had Macy's same determination and ambition despite the parade of 'no's' so prevalent in this business.

When they finally finished casting the movie, Nick yawned. "I'm still jet lagged. Heading back to the hotel."

"See you bright and early Monday morning," said DeMello. "I need you chipper and ready to go. Crew call at six. Casting call at eight for the first production meeting."

"Okay, see you then." Nick wrapped his scarf around his neck and pulled his knit cap down over his sun-lightened hair.

DeMello peered over his cheater glasses at Nick. "I rely on you to keep all the departments playing in the sandbox together. You're the only guy I know who can orchestrate a symphony with gaffer wizards, sound sorcerers, and light warlocks. You have a miraculous way of getting them to work together. You deliver movie magic."

Nick smiled. "I appreciate that, Logan. All it takes is respect. My folks taught me that."

"They taught you right. You've become invaluable to me. I don't want to lose you." DeMello gave him a solemn look.

EVERYBODY LOVES POLAR BEARS

Nick let out an uneasy breath. "Right, I know. Time to go line up my ducks. I'll see you Monday morning. Dark and early." He grinned and headed out the door.

As he stepped into the frigid January air, reminders of the holidays were everywhere in the darkness. Anchorage did it up magnificently, with colorful lights that brightened the entire city. Because of the predominantly dark winter days, most left their decorative lights up long after the holidays. If the city found a way to slap a light on something, they did. Some citizens even decorated their vehicles with lights.

Nick pulled out of the parking lot onto the familiar streets. Anchorage hadn't changed in the five years since he'd left. Few tourists frequented downtown in January, but tonight a few stalwart souls had hopped aboard horse-drawn sleighs for bone-chilling jaunts along downtown streets. He'd missed this post-holiday subdued ambiance.

As Nick drove down Minnesota Drive to the extended stay hotel the production staff would live in for the next month and a half—the movie stars stayed at the luxurious Captain Cook—he thought back over the hundreds who'd shown up to audition.

Several young women had hit on him, as expected. Happened all the time, as everyone was hungry for their big break. He was used to it, but he persisted in keeping a professional demeanor.

Nick had a tough time doing that with Macy Applegate, however. She had an air about her that irritated yet intrigued him. He liked her guts and determination and had sensed her fierce Alaskan independence. This wild place had a unique way of shaping a person.

Tomorrow, he'd take his rental car down the Seward Highway to do some skiing. He loved down-hilling at Alyeska Resort with its breathtaking scenery. He couldn't wait to ride Chair Six to the top that overlooked Turnagain Arm, where the rugged Chugach Range shot up from sea level like giants rising from the deep.

Yep, that's what he'd do. Skiing relaxed him. He'd been wound up tighter than a gnat's ass and needed loosening up. He'd grab a mouth-watering cinnamon roll as big as Alaska from the bake shop in Girdwood before heading up to ski.

His mouth watered just thinking about it.

Chapter 4

Macy sat back, stunned. She squinted at her phone screen to re-read the email. "I don't believe it! They cast me in *Everybody Loves Polar Bears!*"

Julie Burns cheered from the breakfast table between spoonfuls of cereal. "That's fantastic! Did you get a speaking part?"

Macy scrolled through the lengthy email and spotted the cast list. "Not a speaking part. I'm only an extra. Woman Number Six."

"Hey, you're lucky to get cast as an extra. I've talked to some of our best local actors who didn't get cast." Macy's roommate rose from the breakfast table with her empty bowl of cereal.

Macy held up hers, and Julie took it to the sink. "I honestly didn't think they'd cast me after my snarky interlude with that Westwood guy." Macy grimaced. "He kept interrupting and wouldn't let me deliver all my lines. That guy was knotted up so tight, his nuts squeezed inside out."

Julie howled. "Now there's a visual. Yeah, the L.A. people are tense about working up here in our frigid January weather. I hear most of the scuttlebutt working in the wardrobe department."

"Why would they film here in January? Can't they special effect the winter stuff?" This mystified Macy.

"DeMello is stubborn about wanting authenticity for this movie," shrugged Julie.

"That's so cool that you got on the crew," gushed Macy. "You're on a regular salary. I'll only get paid when they call for extras. My boss told me to use my vacation time to work on the movie. When I run out of that, I'll take leave without pay."

"This movie means that much to you?" Julie sat back down at the table with two cups of coffee and set one in front of Macy.

"It's a risk I'm willing to take." Macy poured creamer into her coffee and stirred it. "I really want this, Jules. I was hoping for a speaking part, and I thought my acting in community theater, TV, and radio ads would qualify me. Acting is acting, right?"

"Working on camera differs from onstage acting," said Julie as she sipped her coffee. "You're used to live audiences and belting lines to the back row. You can whisper your lines to a camera," she whispered to emphasize her point.

"It'll take adjustment, but I can do it. Guess I shouldn't have shouted my lines in the audition. I scared the bejesus out of Westwood." Macy chuckled, recalling how he'd sprung off the floor like a startled cat.

"Show these Hollywooders your wonderful talent. Once you wedge your foot in the door, kick it wide open and show them what you're capable of," Julie said definitively.

Macy stared out the window. The sun glinted on the snow like sparkling diamonds. "I'm thinking of going skiing with Andrew. Skiing relaxes me. It'll get rid of my jitters before the first production meeting on Monday." Macy windmilled her arms to loosen them up, taking in the blue sky and the ice crystals floating off tree branches like tiny snow fairies.

"Don't break a leg before it's time to break a leg," said Julie, winking. "Still hanging out with Andrew, huh? Is he still puppy-dogging you to be his girlfriend?"

EVERYBODY LOVES POLAR BEARS

"You know me. When guys zero in for commitment, I'm the artful dodger." Macy furiously danced her thumbs on her phone. "I keep telling him we're only friends, but it doesn't take."

"How do you know he isn't the right one?" asked Julie.

"Andrew is brother material, not boyfriend material. Besides, the one time we hooked up, there were no exploding roman candles. Not even a sparkler. He wants us to move in together." Macy glanced up from her phone. "Like that'll happen."

"Ah, the sticky boyfriend." Julie peered at Macy's phone screen, then she reached over and grabbed the phone. "Maybe you like him more than you're letting on?"

"No way. Seriously, we're just friends," insisted Macy, snatching her phone back.

"I'll say one thing. There are some luscious dudes working on this movie," said Julie, eyes gleaming. "Dylan Ford, hello? His ranking meter on all movie apps shot up vertically overnight when they announced this movie. I need a personal fan strapped to me whenever he's in Wardrobe."

"He is rather hot," said Macy. "But frankly, guys who are in love with themselves don't cut it for me. Even if you hook up with one, he'll toss you back into the groupie pond with the rest of the fish eager to bite his hook."

"With his dangling worm." Julie's eyebrows jumped, and Macy burst out laughing.

The assistant director's face rolled like a ticker across Macy's brain. "That Westwood guy is another one who is in the love-himself category. I bet he French kisses the mirror every morning after he brushes his teeth."

Julie chortled. "We'll be working with more like him, I'm afraid. But hey, we can play them the way they play everyone else, like a chess game."

"I don't want to play anyone. I want film experience so I can get out of Dodge." The minute her words left her mouth, Macy had a stab of guilt. She loved Alaska, but she was in a hometown rut and wanted to break free. This was a way out.

"One lady in my office has a daughter who's a chef at the Captain Cook Hotel," commented Macy. "She said Dylan Ford orders the same thing each morning for breakfast: an egg-white omelet with three farm fresh eggs, diced fresh vegetables, and spinach leaves. And he specifies what kind of extra virgin olive oil to cook it in."

"No kidding?" chuckled Julie. "One of the crew said Victoria Miracle has California fresh fruit and vegetables flown up to Anchorage each day because she freaked out at our green bananas."

"Fresh fruit is already flown up here daily," said Macy, shrugging.

"Yeah, but Ms. Miracle has to have it from her designated growers."

"Geez, picky much?" Macy rolled her eyes as her phone pinged with a notification.

Andrew texted: *Be there in five!*

As Macy tugged on a turtleneck and pulled on her ski pants, excitement bubbled inside her.

I've been cast in the polar bear movie!

One thing crossed her mind: the way the other dark-haired casting director had regarded her when he'd taken her photo. His *I want to do you* look wasn't lost on her. No way would she compromise her morals to gain a foothold in the movie business.

EVERYBODY LOVES POLAR BEARS

Julie snapped her to the present. "Just think, you'll be building professional experience on your home turf without setting foot in Hollywood. Does your email say what they'll pay you?"

Macy tapped it and squinted. "Aside from requiring me to sign a non-disclosure agreement, it says I'll make a little over a hundred bucks a day." She grimaced at her roommate. "I've got to get a bigger part."

Julie smiled. "You've got to start somewhere. This is an excellent stepping stone. Get experience here, create an IMDb page, and slap your resume on it. Then head south to L.A. where you'll knock 'em dead."

"That's what I'm hoping." Macy bent to wriggle a foot into a beige *Xtratuf* boot.

"Westwood is the assistant director. You'll have to charm him if you want a bigger part." Julie gave Macy an impish grin. "My observation so far is that DeMello does pretty much whatever Westwood advises."

Macy wrinkled her nose in distaste and crossed her arms. "I'd rather chew off my arm than stroke Westwood's ego."

"I guarantee there will be some in the cast who will kill to do a charm dance for Westwood. He's hotter than Dylan Ford. You'll have to take a number and get in line if you want Westwood's attention."

Macy shook her head adamantly. "No way. Westwood is the last person on the planet who'll get my attention. You won't see me anywhere near him."

"Uh-huh. We'll see." Julie stood and headed to the bathroom.

"He's a jerk." Macy's resolve became stronger. "No flipping way!" she called out.

"Famous last words!" Julie hollered back.

LOLO PAIGE

Giddy with excitement about the movie, Macy hurried to her room to collect the rest of her ski gear and wait for Andrew.

Chapter 5

Nick skied several exhilarating runs down the slope from Alyeska's Chair Six until the burn of exhaustion in his legs signaled him to take a break. He hadn't skied in subzero temperatures since forever, and the wind chill had sapped his energy in the last muscle-straining run.

He glided towards the lodge known as the Roundhouse, a large octagonal building surrounded by towering spruce trees and glittering snow. He slid to a stop and removed his skis when he heard a melodic voice in an animated discussion with another familiar voice.

He glanced at a flushed face topped by a turquoise stocking cap. The face belonged to Macy Applegate, the woman who'd been so insistent on completing her reading.

"Fancy seeing you here," he said casually.

Macy raised her eyebrows in surprise. "Westwood!" Her gaze dropped to his ski boots. The tip of her nose moved as she furrowed her brow. "Oh, so you Californians ski?"

He gave her an odd look. "Some of the best downhill skiing is in California."

Only an Alaskan would be snobbish about skiing. He sensed it would do no good to elaborate. Instead, he moved to the door and held it open, motioning her inside.

"After you." He thought it was cute how her frosted breath floated up in puffs from her baby doll lips. Her upper lip reminded him of Twin Peaks, a mountain north of Anchorage. Two perfect, kissable peaks—but that was the last thing he should be thinking right now.

"Nick Westwood?" said Macy's eager companion. "Hello, I'm Andrew. You cast me as a reporter for the movie."

"Oh, yes." Nick recognized the man from his audition. This must be Macy's boyfriend, judging by the way he seemed to idolize her.

"You're the last person I expected to see here," she said, entering the octagonal building. "Thought you L.A. types stayed huddled around gas fireplaces in your hotel rooms?"

"Don't have a fireplace in my room." Nick flashed a smile and followed them inside.

All three headed towards the concession counter, where a woman with bright red lipstick and a nose ring stood ready to take their order.

Nick spoke first. "Three hot chocolates, please."

"You must be thirsty," Macy commented, staring straight ahead at the beverage board behind the counter. "Ski quite a few runs?"

"Yes, I did, in fact," said Nick, his gaze lingering on Macy, taking in her every detail. "You and your boyfriend's drinks are on me."

"You don't have to do that," she blurted, her eyebrows lifting. "And Andrew isn't my—" she stopped, seemingly to rethink it. "We've done theater together. We're just cast mates." She twirled her hand in a circular motion, as if trying to extract the words from her mouth.

The server delivered their hot drinks. When Nick retrieved his wallet and opened it, his debit card flopped onto the counter. As he reached for it, Macy's eyes dropped to it. He snatched it and tapped

EVERYBODY LOVES POLAR BEARS

his chip card on the reader. He hoped she didn't note his real name on the card. Like many in Hollywood, he'd changed his name to better fit the film world.

Nick motioned at the two hot chocolate drinks on the counter. "Here you go. Help yourself."

Andrew reached for a cup and gushed, "Thanks, Mr. Westwood. You're very generous. I look forward to working with you."

Nick knew how the game was played. Actors greased the skids to get into higher favor. Andrew wasn't the first, and he certainly wouldn't be the last. Nick wouldn't judge him for it. He hadn't forgotten what it was like when he'd started out.

Macy hesitated, then picked up the other hot chocolate. "You didn't have to do this but thank you."

"You're welcome." He considered apologizing for his behavior in her audition, but if he did that for every actor, he'd drown in a sea of apologies.

Her eyes bored into his, sharp and assessing. "Well, don't get hurt on the mountain. Alaska skiing can be dangerous for outsiders." Her brittle smile softened slightly.

Nick stared back at her, the corner of his mouth twitching. "I'll try not to hurt myself, but thanks for the warning."

Andrew lit up. "Please don't go yet. Why don't you join us first, Mr. Westwood? We can talk about the film."

Nick paused. His first encounter with Macy didn't win him a medal for likeability, yet he didn't want her uncomfortable with his presence.

"Okay... I guess." Macy lifted her shoulder.

"Over here." Andrew motioned them to a table next to a window overlooking the bunny slope. He scooted over to pull a chair out for Nick. "Have a seat."

Andrew's enthusiasm amused Nick, though he noticed a flicker of hesitation on Macy's face. She gave him a fast glance, then looked away.

Nick took a seat. "Congratulations to both of you for getting cast in our movie. Competition was fierce. We didn't expect the hundreds that showed up to audition."

"Why not?" said Macy. "Alaska has an enormous talent pool, and we're extremely proud of it."

"I'm sure you are." Nick bit his tongue. He was keenly aware of the remarkable talents of Alaskans, but he chose not to expand on the subject. Instead, he rubbed his fingertip around the rim of his steaming cup of hot chocolate, noting Macy's sparkling pools of jade and her expressive face, while Andrew boasted about his acting career.

"I can't wait for my scenes with Dylan Ford. He was epic in *Terminal Blast*," gushed Andrew. He went on and on about Ford's performance, as everyone did.

What Nick didn't share was that Dylan had been a nightmare to work with on that movie, and Nick had spent a good deal of his time coaxing a neurotic, hungover Dylan from his trailer to film scenes.

Macy patted Andrew's arm. "Andrew is one of our best actors. He's been in several Equity productions and has toured the lower forty-eight with them."

"As I recall, you had a strong audition." Nick said this to every actor he cast. What Nick remembered about Andrew was that he hadn't stopped bragging about himself. But that hadn't been a reason not to cast him. His type did well on camera because they had confidence and hungered for the chance to be a movie star.

"Is it true that once we're on the set, we can get a bigger role?" Andrew's eagerness was at fever pitch. Nick thought he might levitate off his chair.

Nick shrugged. "Sometimes. If you hit your marks and take direction well." He rubbed his finger up and down his cardboard cup of cocoa, trying not to ogle Macy.

Andrew nodded before quickly changing the subject. "I saw you skiing up on top. You carve slopes like you know these runs inside and out."

"This is my first time here," lied Nick. "I mostly ski in California and Colorado." He pointed to his stocking cap, with "Aspen" embroidered across it.

"That's cool." Andrew laughed nervously. "I bet you know a lot of famous people in Aspen." He waited expectantly.

Nick sipped his cocoa. He refrained from name-dropping, though it would be fun to see Andrew's eyes pop out if he mentioned knowing Sarah Palin. And Cher.

"What can we expect at tomorrow's production meeting?" asked Macy in a matter-of-fact tone.

"We'll do an orientation, so everyone knows what to expect. Familiarize everyone with film terminology," he responded.

"Alaskans aren't hicks. We know our way around film sets," she said icily. "You aren't the first people to come up here to film a movie." Her terse demeanor enveloped him like hoar frost. "They filmed *The Frozen Ground* up here with Nicolas Cage and John Cusack, if you recall."

"I didn't come up to work on that one." He was trying to be friendly, but her terse attitude blew past him like an arctic breeze.

Nick noticed Macy scrutinizing him. Was that a glint of amiability in her eyes? *Right. She can't stand me.* He'd received her negative vibes loud and clear. Her animosity radiated toward him in waves.

"See you on set," chirped Andrew, practically bouncing in his seat. His enthusiasm was like a kanga, excited to take its first leap across Australia's Outback.

"I'd better get going." Nick rose from the table and aimed his cup to pitch it in the trash. "It'll be dark driving back to Anchorage, so watch out for moose."

Rut-Roh.

It was out of his mouth without thinking. He didn't want anyone to know he was born and raised in Alaska for fear of being perceived as naïve and unsophisticated by the power players in the L.A. film business. He'd received advice early on to keep quiet about his Alaskan background.

Macy narrowed her gaze. "As a Californian, how would you know about moose on our roads up here?"

"That's all I've heard from the locals," he rushed to explain. "We have wildlife on our roads in California, too, so I know the drill. See you both tomorrow morning." Nick flashed her a smile and headed toward the door for a fast exit.

Once in the changing room, he clunked over to a bench to exchange his ski boots for a pair of *Xtratuf* boots.

Nick would bet on a royal flush what must be spinning around inside Macy's brain: those new to Alaska wouldn't routinely utter caution about moose, unless they'd had a run-in with one. He chastised himself, wondering how long he could keep up his masquerade. It was easy to do back in L.A. Out of sight, out of mind. But now that he was back home, it could be more of a challenge. He'd have to think twice before running off at the mouth.

No one wanted to give a chance to someone from nowhere Alaska, when they had the option of experienced professionals from New York, Chicago, or L.A. To make things easier, he claimed L.A. as his birthplace since he was already familiar with the city.

As Nick made his way back along the Seward Highway, a light snow brushed his windshield. He recalled the winters of snow machining in the Caribou Hills; the fun summers on the Kenai Peninsula where he'd grown up—the king salmon he'd caught as a kid, fish that were taller than he was—and the fields of fireweed and forget-me-nots. He longed for those times with his family, especially with his dad, before the cancer that had stolen his mom. His father was never the same and now lived in assisted living in southern California, where Nick visited him regularly.

Nick reached the extended stay hotel he shared with the production crew and unlocked his room door with a sigh of relief, thankful for the quiet time to himself. He needed to regroup and prepare for tomorrow morning's cast and crew orientation at the first production meeting.

Pulling off his boots and arranging them near the room heater, Nick made straight for the kitchenette and popped open an Alaskan Amber to take the edge off after spending the day on the slopes. The cold brew slid down his throat, soothing it.

He was antsy to get started on this movie so he could head back to California, where he belonged—because he sure didn't belong in Alaska anymore.

Chapter 6

Macy stepped through the double doors into Anchorage's West High School gymnasium, taking in the sights and sounds of the excited crowd. Along one wall people sat on a row of bleachers, everyone excited about the first production meeting. Macy carefully maneuvered through the throng and chose the aisle seat in a middle row.

She sank onto the hard wooden bleacher, her eyes searching the room. She recognized familiar faces from several theater groups and other friends she'd encouraged to audition for the movie. Her eyes landed on Nick Westwood, a few rows down on the gym floor. He was deep in a conversation with Dylan Ford.

He'd dressed himself in Alaskan casual, with a long-sleeved Henley and a forest green vest topping extensive legs in tight, faded jeans. How sweet. Still trying to fit in with the locals. Macy wasn't fooled by Westwood's charm and stunning looks. In her view, he was still an arrogant bonehead.

Macy envisioned the Hollywood people sitting in cross-legged yoga poses before the meeting, discussing what to wear: Victoria Miracle and Dylan Ford deciding to sport their designer threads from Rodeo Drive, thumbing their noses at Alaskan casual.

Director Logan DeMello took center stage and fiddled with his mic. "Is this thing on?" The gym speakers emitted a deafening, high-pitched screech, causing everyone to cringe. Someone rushed over to assist the director, and the sound stopped.

EVERYBODY LOVES POLAR BEARS

"Well, I guess it's on. Welcome, everyone, to *Everybody Loves Polar Bears!*" he boomed into the mic, his voice reverberating around the gym.

Boisterous cheers went up from the enthusiastic audience of cast and crew.

DeMello continued. "First, let me introduce our cast. The first two need no introduction. Unless you've been living underground, you know about our last movie, *Terminal Blast*..." He paused for effect, while the crowd erupted into cheers and applause.

"This gentleman needs no introduction, but I'll do it, anyway. Meet America's favorite heartthrob, Dylan Ford!" While DeMello waited for America's hottest box office star to saunter up next to him, the entire gym erupted into a chorus of whistles and thunderous applause.

"We love you, Dylan!" yelled women all over the gym.

Dylan stood next to DeMello, modestly placing a hand on his heart and offering a slight bow to show his appreciation.

"His dazzling leading lady certainly needs no introduction," DeMello said into his mic. "I'm sure you remember her recent role in *The Worldly Assassin*. May I present the lovely and talented Victoria Miracle, our marine scientist in *Everybody Loves Polar Bears!*"

The audience erupted in more cheers, applause, and whistles as Victoria waved on her way to stand next to Dylan Ford. Macy clapped along with everyone else but was too stunned to whistle and yell. They cast sexy Victoria as a marine scientist to save the polar bears?

Macy had looked her up online. Victoria had played a stripper in her last movie, which hadn't done well at the box office. Before that, she played a nurse running from a serial killer with her uniform conveniently torn and unbuttoned, kissing her rescuer on the run. In another film, she played a seductive Irish assassin, but her mangled Irish accent had been cringeworthy. Macy couldn't envision Victoria playing a credible scientist.

Dylan and Victoria stood next to the movie director, waving at their adoring fans and milking it, then returned to their perch on the front bench. DeMello introduced a few well-known supporting actors who stood to wave, then sat back down.

"And now for my illustrious crew. Most of you have already met Mr. Nick Westwood, my right-hand man. He's the A.D., or assistant director. He oversees most everything on this production, and what he says goes." He motioned Westwood to come forward.

This elicited an excited response from the women in the audience as they whooped, hollered, and whistled while Westwood ambled out to join the cast and crew lineup.

"Give me a break," muttered Macy.

"What's the matter?" Andrew had seated himself next to her.

"Nothing." Macy couldn't believe the amount of adoration thrown at Nick Westwood. They may as well be tossing roses at his feet.

As Westwood stood beside the movie director, women were on their feet with hands clasped to their chests, throwing playful kisses at him. Nick greeted the roomful of enthusiasm with his panty-melting smile as DeMello gave him the mic.

Look at him, all cocky and condescending beneath his form-fitting Henley, outlining every muscle in his chest. He's a disgrace to Henleys, she thought bitterly.

"Good morning, everyone. Like Director DeMello said, I'll be your go-to guy for anything you need. We've emailed you the film

EVERYBODY LOVES POLAR BEARS

schedule, but if you'd like a hard copy, raise your hand, and we'll get someone to bring you one."

Macy's arm flew up, purely out of spite, even though she already had the electronic version.

Nick's gaze shot up to Macy's resting witch face, but his megawatt grin didn't waver as he motioned for someone to bring her a paper copy. A woman scurried up to Macy with a film schedule, and Macy nodded a thank you.

"Your department heads will see to your needs and will answer your questions once we start filming. But just so you know, the buck stops with me," said Westwood, pointing at himself.

"Sure it does," Macy's comment dripped with sarcasm.

Andrew jabbed her with his elbow. "What's the matter? You don't like the assistant director? He paid for our hot chocolate yesterday at Alyeska."

"He gave me a hard time at my audition," she said grumpily.

"At least you got cast," said Andrew. "Isn't that what you wanted?"

"Uh-huh." Macy flipped through the film schedule, searching for her name. When she found it, her stomach dropped. There it was: Unit C, the lowest rung on the movie ladder. She was a background extra. Woman Number Six. Well, it was better than Woman Number Twenty-Six. She was human scenery.

At least there was one thing she was thankful for—with any luck, she wouldn't have to deal with the dickwad assistant director.

Westwood motioned at the front row of production staff to stand and join him for introductions. "Julie Burns is the wardrobe guru for this movie. Come forward, Julie, so everyone knows who you are."

Macy stood to whoop and holler for her bestie roommate, who waved and beamed back at her.

Westwood gestured to a woman in a multi-colored caftan. "This is Sylvia, the extras supervisor. She has minions who'll wrangle extras in each unit. Each of you will get a security ID. Don't lose it because you won't get on set without it."

Nick held up his phone. "And please, everyone, absolutely no cell phones on the set. If we see you taking photos, we'll take your phone, delete them, and boot you out the door. We can easily replace you. Be sure to uphold your NDA agreement. What happens on set stays on set." He pointed at the cell phones still aimed at him. "Starting now."

To Macy's amusement, all cell phones quickly lowered and magically disappeared. She laughed outright as Westwood glanced up, his eyes staying on her as he made the next comment.

"Stay positive, but above all, please be patient. There's no shortage of hurry-up-and-wait time when filming a movie." Everyone applauded.

Westwood could tell this audience to go to hell and they'd enjoy the trip, thought Macy, bristling that he'd aimed his comment at her.

Is he insinuating I'm impatient and have a negative attitude?

DeMello checked the wall clock. "Okay, everyone, we've listed film locations on your schedules. We'll see you bright and early tomorrow for our first day of filming. Check in, then report to hair, makeup, and wardrobe. Above all, have fun! See you in the movies!"

A cheer went up, and the room buzzed with excitement from the crowd of mostly Alaskans as they made their way out of the gym, talking and laughing.

EVERYBODY LOVES POLAR BEARS

"Guess I won't be seeing you, since I'm a Unit C loser," grumbled Macy, stepping outside to the snowy sidewalk, the weight of disappointment heavy on her shoulders. The bottoms of her boots crunched loudly as they bit into the cold snow.

"Put in a good word for me if you get a chance," she said glumly, beeping an angry command to her Toyota to fire up its engine. Instead, she pressed the panic button and her car screamed bloody murder from the middle of the parking lot.

"Damn it! I hit the wrong freaking button!" Breaking into a frosty-breathed run, Macy beelined toward the flashing lights and obnoxious beeping. She reached her car and fumbled with her key fob, finally shutting off the miserable racket. She turned around with folded arms, staring down at the snowy ground.

"Mace, you look like you lost your last friend," consoled Andrew as he slipped an arm around her. "Once they see your amazing talent, you'll get a bigger part." His other hand lifted her chin. "Give us that positive smile."

She contorted her face into an absurd expression with a mannequin grin.

Andrew's smile deepened into laughter, and he gave her a sideways hug. "See you tomorrow, Woman Number Six." He climbed into his vehicle and pulled out.

"Rub it in, why don't you?" muttered Macy, beeping the key fob to unlock her door just as a stretch limousine pulled up behind her car.

"Oh, great, not again!" she lamented, raising her arms and dropping them to her sides as she glared at the limo.

A window slid down halfway. "What's an excellent restaurant around here?"

Macy's eyes widened as she took in Dylan Ford in the flesh. He was so bundled up, she hardly recognized him; he looked more like a snowman on steroids. She noted the faux fur on his brand spanking new Alaskan parka, with matching earmuffs and a cashmere scarf hiding most of his handsome face.

"Um, sure...we have Table Nine, which is hugely popular, and Wolf's Tooth Brewpub," she stammered in disbelief, her breath misting in the frigid air as she struggled for composure. Why on earth was this legendary film icon talking to *her?*

"I want a place with exceptional food where no one recognizes me." His eyes smiled at her.

"That's a tall order." Macy swallowed a laugh. "Sorry, but you're in the wrong town for that. People around here can't get enough of action movies, especially *Terminal Blast*. Good movie, by the way," she gushed.

"Thanks. That's kind of you to say." He studied her for a moment. "Want to have lunch with me?" His question zinged her like a fast hockey puck.

Macy's mind sped to her resolution about not sprawling on a casting couch to work her way up the film ladder. "Um, I... well, I have an appointment, so I can't," she forced out against her will, her heart somersaulting. She moved close to the limo and displayed her phone. "But here are some options."

"Thanks, I appreciate that." Dylan Ford lowered his scarf to offer her his billion-dollar L.A. smile. "Are you sure you don't want to come?"

"I really can't. But thanks, anyway," she said, aghast at herself for saying it.

EVERYBODY LOVES POLAR BEARS

"What a shame. See you on the set." His gaze lingered on her as the limo sped off.

Macy watched in baffled silence, thinking herself insane for turning down a lunch invitation from a famous movie star. Apparently, her moral compass had stubbornly overruled his invitation. He wouldn't have seduced her in the limo, would he? Macy pondered that one for a moment, then started her car.

For gosh sakes, it was only lunch. Don't be paranoid.

As her Highlander warmed up, Macy danced her thumbs in a text to her roommate.

You'll never guess who asked me to lunch?!!!

Julie responded. *Let me guess. Westwood?*

Nice try! Dylan Ford! Macy typed several emojis with surprised expressions.

Shut up! Julie texted back. *Are you going?*

No. Macy waited for the fallout. It flew back in a heartbeat.

Why??? Are you out of your mother-effing mind?!

Instead of replying, Macy grimaced and tossed her phone onto the passenger seat. She couldn't believe she'd turned down Dylan Ford's invitation. Maybe she *was* out of her mind. Yet her gut instinct urged her not to go. She pointed her car toward her South Anchorage condo, her mind lingering on the production meeting.

Nick Westwood's image crept into her head. As much as she tried to shove it back out, she couldn't help but recall his generosity at the ski area, as well as the broad smile that he'd beamed up at her in the bleachers.

Macy flashed back to yesterday at the concessions counter when Westwood dropped his credit card. It had surprised her to catch the name "Andreanoff" before he picked it up. She thought it was strange, but that was probably the name on the expense account for the film production.

Shaking off thoughts of Westwood, Macy reminded herself she didn't have to like everyone involved with the film. All she needed to do was stay professional and get along with everyone in the sandbox.

Although Westwood's charming smile had softened her a bit during the production meeting, she refused to let down her guard. Despite her efforts to resist, she found herself reluctantly drawn to his rugged charm. This both bewildered her and ticked her off. He may be pretty, but the guy had the personality of a bull moose in rut.

She'd remind herself of that fact whenever she encountered him during the filming of this movie. Beautifully wrapped packages weren't always an indicator of what was inside.

And this gorgeous package was certainly no exception to the rule.

Chapter 7

Nick hurried from the production meeting, mentally juggling a multitude of tasks before the start of filming tomorrow. He hurried toward the parking lot before anyone could flag him down.

He'd zeroed in on Macy when he stood to address the cast and crew. She had one of those faces that set her apart from a crowd. Her cheeks had a rosy hue, and her eyebrows arched in a perpetual state of curiosity, showcasing bright emerald eyes. Wavy, auburn hair fell past her shoulders.

Despite her surly attitude toward him, he'd been delighted to learn Andrew wasn't her boyfriend when they'd bumped into each other at the Alyeska ski resort. Did that mean she wanted Nick to know she was single and available?

Don't jump to conclusions. She despises you, he scolded himself as he climbed into his luxury rental SUV with the dark-tinted windows.

Dylan Ford's limo stopped behind Macy Applegate's car, a few parking spaces away, with his window slid partway down.

Nick let out an irritated sigh.

Here we go again. Mr. Smooth Operator wastes no time moving in on the local beauties. The 1980s *Sade* song played in his head as he settled in to watch Ford in action.

Nick toyed with interrupting the movie star's flirtation, but he hesitated, curious to see how Macy would handle it. He slid his window down, then ducked into low-rider mode in the driver's seat. Icy air tinged his ears as he strained to listen.

Sure enough, Dylan asked where a good place for lunch was, his worn-out pickup line. Nick mouthed the words along with him since he'd observed this infamous box office star hitting on local women in the last few productions. Macy suggested a few restaurants, and true to fashion, Dylan promptly asked if she wanted to come along.

What a dinkwad.

"Okay, Applegate, are you going to sell out and play up to The Talent for your big break?" Nick muttered at the windshield, squinting to see if Macy would bite Dylan's hook.

"Um, I... well, I have an appointment, so I can't," Macy's words floated into Nick's ears, and he let out a happy lungful of air.

"Good woman," he mumbled, frosty breath filling his headspace.

Macy got into her red vehicle, leaving a stupefied Dylan-Hot-Dick gaping after her.

"Too bad, sucker." Nick closed his window and laughed as the limo sped off. He cranked the engine and drove to his extended stay hotel in Anchorage's midtown.

As soon as Nick entered the lobby, he was surprised to see DeMello already there. He motioned Nick over. "Can I have a word?"

Nick's chest tightened. This was DeMello speak for, "Houston, we have a problem." He let out a sigh. "All right, hit me."

"Sylvia's dad had a heart attack last night, and she flew home. You'll need to fill in as the extras' wrangler on Unit A until she either returns or I hire a new one," said DeMello, flicking his eyes to Nick. "We need someone with experience."

EVERYBODY LOVES POLAR BEARS

"So, hire a new one."

"By the time I find one, Sylvia will probably be back. I need you to fill in for her," DeMello said with finality.

Nick held up his hand. "Whoa, wait a minute. So, I'll be juggling assistant director responsibilities *and* cat-herding hundreds of extras? Why don't you have golden boy Josh wrangle the extras? Make him work for a change."

"Westwood, I've seen you juggle cats and rattlesnakes to keep our film schedules on track. Filming in Alaska is expensive, and I can't afford to slow this project. Each day costs thousands, you know that."

Nick groaned and ran his fingers through his hair. "Can't we hire someone local for this? Surely, there is someone experienced here in Alaska." Nick raked his brain for existing contacts.

"Yes, if this were a small production," said DeMello. "But with all these extras, I need someone who's an expert with crowd control and who won't let us get bogged down. Right now, that someone is you. If Josh did it, we'd have chaos."

"Wish I was an executive producer's son so I could get a free pass," groused Nick.

DeMello eyed him over his cheater glasses. "Need I remind you that the Writer's Guild of America is in negotiation talks with the Alliance of Motion Picture and Television Producers? We must get this movie filmed in case negotiations fail and the WGA strikes. We cannot cross a picket line."

"I'm well aware," Nick responded. The situation had been dangling over their heads for months, and DeMello constantly pressured everyone to work at the speed of light to finish their projects so they could finish filming the polar bear movie in case a strike was to occur.

"Remember how they flogged the dinosaur supervisor in that T-Rex movie? They said he had one job. You don't want to be that guy." DeMello said it in jest, but Nick's stomach flopped, knowing his workload had just quadrupled.

"Yeah, poor Phil," Nick said drily.

"Be a sport and do this for me." DeMello patted Nick's forearm. "I'll make sure you are well compensated. I'll get you your own movie to direct."

Nick groaned inwardly. *Here we go again. The same old song and dance—do as I'm asked, and something will come of it... maybe.*

Reluctantly, he uttered the same magic words he'd said a thousand times before. Maybe this time would be different. He could only hope. "Okay. You can count on me."

"That's my boy. Now go rest up. I've texted you a laundry list of things for you to take care of for tomorrow. Crew call is at five, three hours earlier than casting call, so make sure you're ready."

Nick wolfed down the sandwich he'd grabbed on the run. Once he settled into his hotel room, he showered and relaxed on his bed, flipping through channels on the TV.

His thoughts returned to Macy. Maybe he'd ask her out for dinner? DeMello insisted that crew members refrain from dating cast members during a production. In his mind, it was an unaffordable distraction and affected everyone's professionalism on set.

"What am I doing? I'm the death star. She hates me!" muttered Nick. "I'm no better than Dylan Ford." With a sigh of resignation, he clicked off the TV and shoved the notion from his brain.

EVERYBODY LOVES POLAR BEARS

At this point in his life, he yearned more for companionship than anything else. But he wouldn't fish off the company pier just because it was convenient. He was here for work, not pleasure.

I'll only be here three weeks. Don't get involved with the local talent. I need to stay focused and professional. Do my job and go home.

When he thought of home, a roiling mix of guilt and sadness crept in. Alaska would always be home, but he'd distanced himself from his roots to establish credibility. Denying Alaska felt traitorous. Then again, what was home? Was it Alaska, where he'd grown up, or was it Los Angeles, his home for the past five years?

Alaska wasn't home anymore, and Macy Applegate wasn't an option.

Now if he could only talk himself into believing those things.

Chapter 8

On her first day of filming, Macy shivered near the edge of an open water pond the crew had created under a municipal film permit in Anchorage's industrial section near the Port of Anchorage.

The crew called it Polar Pond, where they filmed scenes with polar bears in the water, simulating the ocean with ice floes. Mixed in with real ice were chunks of Styrofoam, cleverly disguised to blend in.

The movie crew had sawed through the ice to create open water for the animatronic polar bear the props crew had created for the production. Someone had piled snow around the edge of the pond to make it look more like the Arctic Ocean and less like a backyard swimming pool.

Ten extras, including Macy, formed a semi-circle around the dark water as the sun hung low in Alaska's winter sky. A biting January wind had everyone bundled to the teeth, fitting for a movie scene taking place in the Arctic. The breeze gusted spindrift into their eyes.

Macy had read the scene where Victoria's character had reunited the cub with his mother after being separated during a severe winter storm. The script intended this scene as a touching moment with humans helping the bears.

She eyed the pond with a skeptical eye. No way was she going anywhere near that water with those large ice chunks bobbing

EVERYBODY LOVES POLAR BEARS

around—too many horror stories about people and snow machines falling into icy water, never making it out again.

"Okay folks, here's the deal," said the chunky Unit C director with his dark beard and a paunch that stretched his zipped jacket. Macy remembered him from Westwood's crew introductions at the production meeting. 'Zippo' was embroidered on his backwards baseball cap, and she wondered how he could stand the biting cold without covering his forehead.

"All of you extras are either reporters or scientists." He glanced up at a bespectacled woman standing off set with an 'Animal Protection' name tag that hung around her neck as she huddled in her long down coat. "We have enough animal protection people."

Zippo motioned to a nearby truck. "Baby Snowflake is an orphaned polar bear cub loaned to us from a conservation group. Don't worry, his handler has complete control over the cub." He flashed an amiable smile at the animal protection woman, who dipped a prim nod in response. "These scenes will be inter-cut, with Dylan Ford playing a local politician and Victoria as the bear scientist."

"You mean she's a marine biologist," corrected Macy, eyeing the caged cub. "I work for an agency involved in polar bear research," she added quickly.

Zippo gave her a blank look. "Uh-huh. Thanks for that piece of information." He pointed his thumb over his shoulder. "That's Fake Mother Snowflake, our animatronic polar bear. We'll lower her into this open pond and direct her movements with remote control." He gestured at the inky pond.

"Oh, so he's like a furry *Jaws*," quipped Macy, eyeballing the dark, frigid water with the scattered ice chunks.

"Extras, please form a semi-circle around the pond. Reporters on the left, and marine biologists to the right." Zippo emphasized it for Macy's benefit. He motioned to an older man with a long gray ponytail. "Distribute your box of goodies, Ozzie."

The bow-legged props guy toddled over to Macy. "Reporter or scientist?"

"Reporter," she replied.

He handed her a fake microphone. "Who's your cameraman?"

"Me." A short, bald guy popped up next to Macy. He reeked of an all-night binge, his bloodshot eyes a crimson roadmap.

Ozzie offered him a large TV camera. "Hold this on your shoulder, like they did back in the eighties," he instructed. "And stick with your reporter."

"Aye-aye, sir!" the inebriated man snapped a salute, which was more like a sporadic dance move than a show of respect. He swayed like a palm tree in a hurricane with a goofy look on his face.

Macy caught a whiff, and it nearly curled her toes. She didn't see the ID tag they were required to wear around their necks, but Zippo had instructed everyone to tuck them under their coats during filming.

"Are you sure you can handle this? You aren't supposed to drink on the job."

"You betcha," he hiccuped, tipping backwards.

Macy grasped his elbow to keep him from falling over. She sent an exasperated look to Zippo, who appeared oblivious to the man's obvious drunkenness.

Zippo climbed onto a seat perched on the long arm of a crane that extended several feet over the water. He grumbled, fiddling with his camera.

EVERYBODY LOVES POLAR BEARS

"It's minus five. Your camera is likely frozen," called out Macy. "Just give it a smack. That usually does the trick with small planes and cars, so why not a camera?"

"This equipment is a tad more sensitive. You can't smack digital. You unplug it and re-plug it." Zippo flicked his eyes up at her. "But thanks for the technical tip and the weather report," he muttered, his voice dripping with sarcasm.

"Just trying to help. Excuse me, but..." Macy pointed at the inebriated bald guy. "Is this person part of the cast?"

"He must be. No one gets in here without going through security." Zippo turned to peer through his camera monitor. "Everyone ready? Get Baby Snowflake over here. Where's Victoria?"

A tall pink neon Barbie hurried toward them, long blonde curls springing up and down like miniature slinkies. Victoria Miracle approached in all her glittery goose-down glory, a fusion of glamour and frostbite protection, reminding Macy of a disco-themed northern lights display. Winter followed her around like a trusty sidekick, along with her entourage of three scurrying behind her.

Macy got a kick out of The Talent and how they expected everyone to dote on them and cater to their every need. Victoria's demeanor was a stark contrast to the independent nature of women Macy knew in Alaska. She'd read about the coddled movie star stereotype, and here was one in the flesh.

"Make this quick. I'm freezing my tush off." The movie star's frosty breaths puffed out of her like a high-speed locomotive.

As Victoria strategically positioned herself next to the pond, Macy couldn't help but imagine her strutting down the runway of a 1960s psychedelic fashion show. Her flashy style was part Picasso, part Gucci, and all sass. Like the Las Vegas Strip at midnight, Victoria stood out in this winter wonderland, her presence impossible to ignore.

Macy bet Victoria never met a camera she didn't like.

The animal handler stood by, holding a long leash attached to the little polar bear cub. He gingerly placed the leash in Victoria's hand, mumbling instructions to hold on tight.

The fish-out-of-water movie star gave Macy a critical up-and-down assessment. "Are you from here? Have you been around bears?"

Macy shrugged. "I know what to do around black and brown bears."

Victoria gave her a look of appraisal. "Good enough for me." She called out to Zippo. "Keep this bear woman next to me at all times." A makeup artist appeared, dabbing lip gloss on Victoria's already shiny lips and arranging her flawlessly spiraled curls. The artist hurried off again.

Zippo ordered the animatronics operator to dunk Mother Snowflake. The operator slowly lowered the crane, placing the fake bear into the water. "We'll edit the crane out later," he announced to no one in particular.

"Vicky, say your lines, then squat next to the little bear and deliver the rest. And don't scare him," directed Zippo from his perch on the crane arm. "We need a tender moment, with Fake Mother Snowflake watching."

Macy couldn't help herself. "Excuse me, hate to keep interrupting, but that wouldn't happen in real life. The mother bear would attack the human to protect her cub. She wouldn't just sit still and watch."

EVERYBODY LOVES POLAR BEARS

"This isn't real life. It's the movies," Zippo said flippantly. "We do what we want in a movie. Now, can we get on with this, please? It's a tad nippy out here, and I'd like to get this done, if you don't mind." He turned away to talk on his headset.

"Don't get your panties in a twist," mumbled Macy.

Victoria chortled. "Love your style, Bear Woman."

Zippo cocked a brow. "Are we ready now, ladies?" He turned to the crane operator. "Lower the fake Mother Snowflake into the water. Quiet, everyone. Rolling. Marker!" He peered through his camera monitor.

A woman held up a black-and-white clapboard in front of the camera. "Scene fourteen. Take one!"

Zippo nodded at the red digital readout and the person snapped it and hurried away.

He pointed at the extras. "Background, action! Victoria, go!"

While Macy and her merry band of extras gathered around Victoria, the drunk guy holding Macy's prop news camera stumbled over.

"Where's my news reporter? Oh! There you are," he slurred, beholding the glorious Victoria. "Hey, you wanna see my oosik?" He swung around and bumped the unsuspecting bear cub on the head.

"Your what?" Victoria wrinkled her face just as the frightened cub bawled and ran in circles around her, wrapping his leash tightly around her legs.

"Get this savage beast away from me!" she yelled. Her legs lashed together as she teetered toward the icy water. "Somebody! Get this leash off me!"

Macy sprinted forward. Her ninja-like reflexes prevented Victoria from tumbling off the edge, but in the process, Macy slipped on the ice-crusted snow. Her feet fought for traction, but it was a losing battle. She lost her balance and flailed wildly, teetering backwards. Arms spinning like windmills, she failed to restore equilibrium and executed a flawless butt-first plunge into the chilly water, like a clumsy duck on a crash landing.

The shock blasted her as icy water swallowed her like a cavernous glacier. Her mammalian diving reflex forced her to gasp, sucking water into her lungs. She sunk a good foot below the surface until her feet hit bottom. She frantically pushed off to get her nose and mouth above water.

The pond wasn't deep, but it was more than Macy's five-feet-two inches. The ice-laden water felt like thousands of icicles drilling into her brain. Her feeble attempt to tread water got her nowhere fast as the frigid water paralyzed her. She was a strong swimmer, but the subzero cold sapped every ounce of her strength.

Screams and shouts gurgled in Macy's ears as she struggled to keep her nose and mouth above the surface. While she bobbed, frosty breaths puffed from panicked mouths as everyone scrambled to get her out.

An inebriated voice hollered, "Get the polar bear to save her!"

Macy's bulging eyes glimpsed Fake Mother Snowflake sitting placidly in the water, staring into the sunset. She wished the animatronic bear could swim over to rescue her.

"I have a dip net in my car!" someone shouted.

Someone else called out, "Hang on, Macy! We'll get you out!"

She couldn't move, like rigor mortis had swooped in early.

A cacophony of voices echoed. "You're gonna need a bigger net! Get her before she goes under again!"

I don't want to die! I have a movie to make!

EVERYBODY LOVES POLAR BEARS

Macy's body sank of its own accord, water gurgling in her ears. Something yanked her, then tugged her through the screaming-cold water.

"Help me here!" A man shouted.

Someone grabbed Macy to lift her, but all she wanted was to sleep.

"Leggo!" she slurred, coughing.

A hand slapped at her cheek, but she barely felt it. "Macy, stay awake! Somebody get my damn vehicle over here now!" The voice had a familiar tone, but felt distant, like it echoed up to her from a deep, glacial crevasse.

Macy's eyelids glued shut. She had a strange sensation of floating through space. She couldn't feel a thing. *Where am I?*

"Sleep," she mumbled, her words sounding like a dying computer battery.

"Stay awake!" the distant voice commanded.

"I can't..." She tried to form words, but her mouth wouldn't work.

"Look at me!" The voice faded.

Is someone holding my face?

Her world turned gray. Then everything went dark.

Chapter 9

Nick Westwood barked orders. "Zippo, start my car and crank the heat! Get me a sleeping bag and some blankets. Most Alaskans have them in their cars." He tossed Zippo his key fob, then picked Macy up off the snow and carried her to his SUV in the nearby parking lot.

Her skin had already turned blue.

Zippo beeped the car unlocked, then opened the tailgate and crawled in to fold down the rear seats.

Nick gently laid Macy inside as Zippo moved up front to start the car. "Zip, cancel the shoot. Send everyone home. I don't want people standing around gawking."

Nick's specialty in handholding was the reason he found himself here, after Victoria's text about her anxiety filming in the extreme cold. While DeMello directed a Unit-A scene, Nick had driven over to placate Victoria.

Zippo dipped a quick nod. "I called nine-one-one to get the paramedics here ASAP."

"We can't wait on them. This woman is already hypothermic and her core needs warming *now*. Good thing my car is still warm from driving over here." Nick removed his coat and tossed it inside. He crawled into the back, and Zippo slammed the tailgate door closed.

"Macy, can you hear me? I'm going to warm you up," said Nick. He didn't like her blue skin color. Not a good sign.

EVERYBODY LOVES POLAR BEARS

Macy's body shook violently, causing her breath to rattle in her chest. Nick rolled her onto her side, so she'd spit out water. Hopefully, she hadn't swallowed too much. She wasn't underwater that long, but long enough to plummet her body temperature.

He had to work fast. Hypothermia was life-threatening and nothing to screw with. It wasn't good that Macy wanted to sleep; she was entering the advanced stages. He had to raise her core body temperature before her brain lost oxygen.

"Julie...I'm tired," mumbled Macy.

Nick's head snapped up. "Macy, it's Nick. Listen to me. You're hypothermic. I must get these wet clothes off you." He kneeled next to her and cursed when his head bumped the vehicle's ceiling. He wished this damn rental were bigger—then again, he hadn't planned on stripping down a woman in his luxury SUV.

He tugged off Macy's saturated stocking cap and mittens, then rolled her from side to side to remove her dripping-wet parka, one sleeve at a time. He eased the drenched coat from under her and tossed it.

Nick tugged Macy's wool sweater up and over her head, then wrestled with her blue turtleneck. She'd dressed for the extreme cold, but it was working against her now. He lifted her saturated turtleneck off, revealing a bright pink bra. He lightly tapped her cheeks and vigorously rubbed her arms.

Not enough. The fastest way to heat her body was with his own.

"Macy, stay awake!" he commanded.

"I can't!" she heaved out. Even when she was out of it, she was obstinate.

He pressed two fingers to the side of her neck. Weak pulse. He yanked off her *Xtratufs* and wool socks, then wrestled with her damn skinny jeans. He loved how they normally sculpted her, but he hated them now. It was like peeling an unripe avocado. He finally stripped them off and tossed them. They slapped the fogged-up window and slid down.

When he had her down to her bra and underwear, he reached into the front seat, where Zippo had tossed in the down sleeping bag and wool blanket. He unzipped the bag and pulled it over the top of her.

Nick undressed himself down to his briefs and wriggled under the bag next to her. He rolled her onto her side, facing him, and pressed his body tightly against her trembling one. She was shaking so hard she shook his entire body. He grimaced at the wet bra that prevented him from fully transferring his heat to her core.

"Don't hate me for this," he mumbled, reaching around to unclasp her saturated bra. Hell, this was a survival situation, he told himself. He pressed his torso against hers and vigorously rubbed her back while massaging her legs with his bare feet to circulate her blood.

"Macy, can you hear me? Tell me if you can hear me!" If he couldn't raise her core temperature, she'd slip into the danger zone. The car had heated, melting the frosted windows. Nick continued warming the front of Macy's body with his own, then climbed over her to warm her backside.

"Julie?" she slurred. "Lemme sleep..."

"It's Nick. I'm warming you up," he said, as if talking to a child.

"Nick who?" mumbled Macy. She was gradually warming, but he couldn't stop heating her with his body until the ambulance arrived.

Nick had done the same when his brother had rolled his kayak on Tustemena Lake on the Kenai Peninsula years ago. He hadn't thought twice about pressing his warm flesh to his brother's back then—saving his life outweighed modesty—as it did now, with Macy.

It seemed an eternity until Zippo opened the driver's door and hollered, "Paramedics are here! I told them what happened."

"Okay, thanks. Give me a minute. Don't open the tailgate until I knock on the window." Nick lifted his head from under the sleeping bag to see the Anchorage Fire Department's red ambulance truck pulling up next to his SUV. Thank goodness for tinted windows.

Nick crawled out of the bag and tugged his clothes on, then hurriedly shoved his feet into his boots, bypassing the socks.

"Macy, are you still with me?" He lifted the sleeping bag and stroked her cheek. Thankfully, the normal color was gradually returning to her skin.

"So tired," she said in a faint voice. She was still out of it, but hopefully she hadn't entered the advanced stages. He had no idea how much time had passed—fifteen, maybe twenty minutes?

Nick remembered his brother's confusion during hypothermia. Because of that experience, he knew how the brain slowed. It had terrified him back then, but having been through it, Nick remained calm in Macy's situation.

She may despise him, but that wasn't relevant at the moment. Nick zipped up the sleeping bag and swaddled her inside of it, then knocked on the rear window for Zippo to open the tailgate.

"Got her warmed up. She needs a saline drip," Nick informed the paramedics as he climbed out. He reached inside to give them Macy's wad of wet clothes. "She'll need these. Sorry, I don't have a bag to put them in."

"The hospital will dry them," the female paramedic responded, taking the clothes from Nick.

The male paramedic grinned at the lacy pink bra dangling from the pile. "Good job, buddy."

Nick gave the guy a disgusted look. "This wasn't exactly a sexual experience."

The guy winked. "Just giving you a hard time. You did the right thing."

"Don't know how right it was, but it was the only option," said Nick.

The two paramedics lifted Macy onto a gurney and slid it into the ambulance.

When the red vehicle pulled out of the mostly empty parking lot, Nick turned to Victoria, who'd strolled over.

"Is Bear Woman all right after that nasty North Pole bath? So much for filming today."

"I'm sure she'll be okay. It was nip and tuck there for a while," replied Nick.

"We'll take another run at this scene tomorrow," said Zippo, joining them.

Nick glanced from Zippo to Victoria. "What the hell happened here? How did one of our extras wind up in the water?"

"It was my fault," Victoria said quickly, pulling her scarf tightly around her neck. Nick had never known Victoria to own up to anything. "Bear Woman saved me from going in."

"Her name is Macy Applegate," said Nick, drawing a coy expression from Victoria, which he ignored.

"An extra bumped Baby Snowflake, and his leash tangled around Vicky," explained Zippo, twirling his finger. "Macy grabbed

EVERYBODY LOVES POLAR BEARS

Vicky to keep her from going in, then fell back-asswards into the water."

Nick's brows shot up. Macy's actions spoke volumes about her character.

The drunk bald guy stumbled up to them, holding a prop camera. "When are we making the movie?" he slurred.

"Who are you?" asked Nick, with a questioning look at Zippo.

Zippo shrugged. "He's the extra who frightened the bear cub and caused the ruckus."

"I'm Skippy," chirped the man. "I'm so sorry. I didn't mean for that pretty lady to fall into the water." A heady whiff of yesterday's dank alcohol hit Nick's nostrils.

Nick blew out air. "It was an accident. But you aren't supposed to be drinking on the job, buddy. Where's your security ID?" Nick peered around the man's shoulder for the security staff, who were supposed to be at the parking lot entrance.

"They didn't give me one. I just walked in." Skippy pointed his thumb at Victoria. "The security guy was busy talking to her." He drew back and gawped at Victoria as if seeing her for the first time. "Hey, you're a movie star! Can I have your autograph?"

"Not right now, honey. My hand will freeze and disintegrate if I take off this mitten." She held it up.

The man's eyes grew wide. "Disintegrate?"

Nick turned to him. "I take it you aren't one of our hired extras. You didn't scare the bear cub on purpose though, did you, Skippy?" Nick made a mental note to chew out security.

"No, I didn't. I swear I didn't." Skippy teetered backwards, and Nick grabbed his elbow. "Steady, pal. You need to sober up."

The gray-haired man's eyes grew round. "Please, sir, I need this job. I don't have food or anywhere to live." He saluted Nick.

"You're homeless? By any chance, did you serve?"

"Air Force. I was an airman at JBER and was in Desert Storm in 1991."

Nick knew how hard it was for homeless people in Anchorage during the winter months. What killed him were the veterans and families with children living on city streets and in the encampments in subzero weather. The situation was far worse than it had been five years ago when he'd left Anchorage.

"Fill out the paperwork and set Skippy up with an ID badge. Get him an extras film schedule for Unit C," Nick ordered Zippo.

"Thank you so much, sir." The man's hands gracefully intertwined in a prayer-like gesture. "I appreciate this so very much."

"Thank you for your service." Nick pointed a finger at him. "But don't drink before you come to work on this film. Understand? Or I'll have to let you go."

The man assumed a penitent expression. "I promise, sir, I won't. I promise." He saluted again.

Zippo raised his brows. "You sure about this, Nick? He's the reason that Macy Applegate fell into Polar Pond."

"What did I just say?" snapped Nick. "Take care of it, Zippo. Get the guy set up. See that he gets a shower and someplace to sleep, while he works on this movie."

"What do I charge it to? DeMello won't want to pay..." Zippo exchanged glances with Victoria.

"Don't worry about DeMello," Nick cut in. "I'll take care of it. Bill it to the production." DeMello was tight with a nickel, but Nick would worry about that later. He'd pay for the expenses with the extras budget.

EVERYBODY LOVES POLAR BEARS

"Sure thing. Okay, come on, pal, let's get warmed up. I have hot tea in my thermos." Zippo took the older man's elbow and steered him toward the parking lot.

"Well, look at you. All soft and squishy, you little teddy bear." Victoria nudged Nick with her elbow. "You aren't the hardass you claim to be. You have a teensy little heart in there, after all." She rubbed her palm in a circle on his chest.

"Two sizes too small, though, right?" His mouth lifted. "I'll take that as a compliment, coming from you. You haven't cut me any slack since I said I wouldn't sleep with you."

"Can't blame me for trying. You made it clear I wasn't the woman for you." She cupped his cheek with her gloved palm. "But the sex would have been fantastic with that hot package I know you have going on under there. Thanks for your honesty about it, by the way," she purred.

"Happy to accommodate." Nick had grown used to Victoria's shameless flirtations. He fished his keys from his pocket. "See you on set tomorrow."

"Good job saving Bear Woman, Aquaman." Victoria lowered her chin with a seductive grin. "I understand that you and she got naked. I envy her."

"I had to get her warm fast." He cocked a brow. "Something tells me you've never taken a first aid class."

"Why would I? I have people to take care of all that." She twirled her gloved hand.

Nick glanced back at Victoria's entourage, sitting in their idling car. "Of course you do." He gave her a direct look. "Keep what happened here to yourself, Vicky, okay? I don't want wagging tongues to distort what happened."

Victoria displayed her cat-eyed look. "You mean, why you got naked with a local actress?"

"Not only that, but I have a feeling Macy won't like how I had to warm her up." He figured he'd have some explaining to do on that score. "To make things worse, she hates me," he added.

"How could anyone not like you? You're adorable. Besides, I have better things to do than to defile your lovely badass reputation." Victoria paused. "You told me you lost a fiancée some time ago. I don't pry, but your sad puppy-dog face wasn't lost on me."

"What's your point?"

"The best way to get over someone is to get on top of someone else. Told you that before, when I tried to get you in bed with me. I could have cured your grief."

"I'm over that now." He mostly was after five years, unless a certain song played on the radio, or a nostalgic memory popped into his mind—the main reason he hadn't been home in a while.

Victoria poked his chest. "Think about what I said. I care about you."

"Thanks." Nick couldn't help but find amusement in Victoria's belief that sex was the solution to every dilemma. He motioned toward the late afternoon salmon-colored sky across Cook Inlet, cloaking Sleeping Lady Mountain with a bright alpenglow.

"This is beautiful lighting to film your scene if you and Zippo are up for it. Get some tight shots with you and Baby Snowflake. Or at least some stills."

Victoria gazed at the red-streaked color palette. "That is actually a clever idea. See? That's why you make the big bucks."

Nick guffawed. "Right. I'm heading back to the ranch."

EVERYBODY LOVES POLAR BEARS

"Why aren't you staying downtown at the Captain Cook with us? You shouldn't be slumming at a three-star hotel. You're the A.D. Plus, I would love it if you were closer. I haven't given up on seducing you," she purred. "Is DeMello seriously that cheap?"

"He wants the crew to congeal. You know, hold hands and sing Kumbaya."

"Well, have fun singing. See you tomorrow, sweetie." Victoria lifted herself to plant a wholesome kiss on his cheek. When she backed up, he eyed her ruby red lipstick and stopped himself from wiping it off. He didn't want to offend her.

If there was one thing Nick excelled at, it was keeping peace in the valley between everyone on a film project. DeMello repeatedly joked that was why he kept Westwood around.

She turned to Nick. "So, what the hell is an oosik?"

Nick gave her an odd look. "Where'd you hear about that?"

"That drunk extra asked if I wanted to see his oosik. I figured he meant, you know, his..." She wiggled her forefinger. "So, what is it?"

Nick stared at Victoria, debating whether to explain that an oosik was the penis bone of a walrus, sometimes up to two feet long. As a result, he'd developed an undying respect for female walruses.

This would undoubtedly gross Victoria out, so he chose the chicken-shit route. "I don't know," he lied, shrugging. "Hey, I have to go. See you later." He was in a hurry to get to the hospital. He wasn't lying about that.

"Okay, later. Bye." Victoria strode over to where Zippo stood, talking to the polar bear cub's handler. "Will someone please tell me what an oosik is?"

Nick shook his head and laughed loudly on the way to his vehicle. Let them explain it to her.

Even though he was exhausted, Nick headed to the hospital to check on Macy before going to his hotel. Hopefully, her roommate would be there by now.

As he turned onto Providence Drive in midtown, one thing Nick knew about Alaska: never take chances with nature's elements. They had a way of sneaking up and threatening a life if a person wasn't careful. There was a saying among the sourdoughs—Alaska had ten ways to kill you every ten minutes.

It was the first day of filming, and the production already had a safety incident. It had to be reported to DeMello. Nick fumbled in his pocket for his phone and punched in DeMello's number while focusing on the road ahead of him. He set his phone in its holder on the dash.

While he waited for his boss to answer, he pointed his car toward the hospital, hoping Macy wouldn't hate him for having pressed his warm, naked body against hers.

Chapter 10

"No! No! Help me!" Macy cried out, gasping for air. Her heart pounded and her body ached. A dull throb pounded her temples. She groaned, trying to sit up, but her muscles protested, and she sank back onto the mattress.

She turned her head, desperate for a grasp on the moment. But her mind only fired blanks.

Where the heck am I?

She stared at the white walls, then her eyes roved out the window to a snowy mountain range painted with a bright pink alpenglow. The room smelled sterile.

"You're finally awake," said a familiar voice.

Macy rolled her head to the other side as it dawned on her that she lay in a hospital bed cocooned in warm blankets.

Nick Westwood sat in a chair next to her bed.

What the heck? Am I seeing things?

She blinked. Shock and awe didn't begin to describe her astonished reaction. Why was Westwood, of all people, sitting next to her bed?

"What are you doing here?" she rasped, her voice barely audible. She coughed, and it hurt like hell.

"How are you feeling?" He smiled, relief clear on his tanned face.

"Like I was rode hard and put away wet," she mumbled, with a hand to her forehead.

"Well, the wet part applies, anyway," he said drily.

"Ow, my lungs hurt." She coughed. "What happened?"

"You stopped Victoria from falling into the pond, then you tumbled in," he replied. "You had all of us worried."

"What time is it?" She noted the darkness outside and glanced around for a clock.

"Late evening. You've been sleeping since this afternoon." He pointed at a nearby table. "The cast and crew got you flowers. Didn't know your favorites."

Macy fixed her gaze on the enormous, multi-colored bouquet. She tried to recall what happened but could only remember snippets... the cub getting tangled... Macy shoving Victoria back. "How is Victoria? And the little polar bear cub?"

"Both are fine," he assured her. "They didn't go swimming like you did."

Her memory slowly returned. "I'm sorry for screwing up the film scene."

"That's the least of our concerns. Accidents happen, especially in this business. You're not the first and won't be the last."

"How did—who pulled me out?" Macy studied him. His presence oddly comforted her.

"I did."

It took a moment for Macy to process that tidbit of information, but the dots still didn't connect.

"I fished you out with a dip-net, then warmed you up in my car."

She stared at him like he'd just landed from Planet Neptune. She untangled the words glomming in her throat. "Did I hear you correctly? A dip net? As in a salmon dip net?" She gaped at him, bewildered. "Where did you get a dip-net in the dead of winter?"

EVERYBODY LOVES POLAR BEARS

"An extra had one stashed in his truck."

"Of course, like any respectable Alaskan after a summer of combat fishing. So, I ended up being the fresh catch of the day." She shook her head in bewilderment. "Then what happened?"

"You became hypothermic, so I had to warm you up in my car until the paramedics arrived. The ambulance brought you here." He motioned at the room with an outstretched arm.

"Wow. Geez, thanks for helping me." The last thing she'd remembered was a vague sensation of floating. Her mind flashed back to the freezing water and the panicked voices. "But I didn't see you there."

"I stopped by to see how things were going at Polar Pond. You impressed our movie star with your heroics. She kept calling you Bear Woman. Were you a grizzly trainer, or were you raised by bears?" he teased.

Macy managed a choking laugh, but it felt like a thousand knives stabbing her lungs. "That would explain my blueberry addiction and my preference for winter hibernation. But in all reality, my bear encounters consist of me playing referee between the black bears and my trash cans between May and September."

"I know what you mean. I used to do that too, down on the—" he stopped, as if catching himself from saying something wrong.

She waited for him to finish. "On the what...?"

"When I...when I'd go, um, camping up at Big Bear, back home in California. Lots of bears up there..." he trailed off.

She peered at him. Was he blushing?

Westwood switched the subject. "Zippo reworked the scene, and he and Victoria finished filming it."

"Oh, good. At least something positive came out of today."

"There's paperwork you'll need to fill out about what happened on set, and our production company will compensate you for all your medical and whatever else. Of course, you may hire an attorney—"

She interrupted. "Wait..." she held up her hand in a stop motion. "What do you mean? Are you presuming I'll sue?"

Westwood shrugged. "People often do in these situations."

"Whoa, just a second." Macy held up her hand. "This isn't *L.A. Law*; this is Alaska. I don't stampede to litigate when these kinds of things happen. I tried to help Victoria and lost my balance, that's all."

"We can discuss this later, after you've had time to recover," he said matter-of-factly. "We have protocols in place for these kinds of incidents. Just wanted you to know."

Macy's head hurt, and she lifted a hand to her forehead. "I'm exhausted. I can't think about all that right now."

"Right. You need rest," he said, rising from his chair. "And we need you back on your feet... when you're able. I'm glad you're all right. I'd better go." He headed for the door.

A wave of exhaustion swept through her, and her heart sped. Sudden anxiety had her afraid to sleep.

"Westwood? Wait, a sec," she rasped.

He turned back. "Please, call me Nick."

"Alright... Nick, can you please stay with me until I fall asleep?" Despite feeling embarrassed about the whole situation, she didn't want to be alone right now after waking from a nightmare where she'd been drowning.

His jaw dropped at her request. "Sure. I can do that." Nick sauntered back to her bedside and dragged the chair closer to her bed. "I'll stay as long as you need."

EVERYBODY LOVES POLAR BEARS

"I know you're busy and all," she said haltingly. "I mean, if you have to be somewhere..."

"No, it's no problem." He waved his hand dismissively. "We've wrapped for the day."

"Tell me a funny story about working on a movie." She rested on her back and closed her eyes.

He chuckled. "I have lots of those."

As Nick talked, Macy figured that falling into an icy pond might not be such a terrible thing after all. It could lead to the start of something else, but to what, she wasn't sure. Her brain was weighty, her eyelids too heavy to lift.

She drifted off to the smooth sound of Nick's voice, his stories about funny things that happened on the set of *Terminal Blast* floating into her ears.

Too bad she couldn't stay awake long enough to hear them.

Chapter 11

Early the next morning, Macy pulled into a parking spot at the film office on 3rd Street in downtown Anchorage. The lazy winter sun hadn't risen yet, but the streetlights cast a sheen on patches of snow and ice, adding sparkles of light as she climbed out of her car.

Sensitive to inhaling the frigid air after yesterday's debacle, Macy tightened her scarf over her nose and mouth, grabbed her ID and purse, and hurried inside. Though polar plunges were popular winter events for Alaskan fundraisers, she'd been unprepared for yesterday's dip. Macy was mostly back to normal, but she was still ultra-sensitive to the January cold. She'd bundled under triple layers beneath her spare parka just to get to work.

Macy's mind drifted to the massive bouquet that overwhelmed her dining room table. Nick Westwood had blown her mind when she woke up to see him in her hospital room. All of yesterday was so surreal.

After Julie had driven her home, Macy sought the comfort of sleeping in her own bed, only to find a naked, uninvited Westwood making cameo appearances in her dreams.

Her cheeks heated as she approached the woman at the check-in desk, irritated at her vivid erotic dreams about a guy she couldn't stand.

"Good morning, checking in for today's filming," said Macy, showing her ID. "I'm with Unit C."

EVERYBODY LOVES POLAR BEARS

The woman squinted at it, then tapped on her tablet with long purple fingernails. "It appears there has been a change. Macy Applegate, right? They've transferred you to Unit A. Here's your new ID."

Macy accepted the new ID, puzzled. "But why...?"

Purple Fingernails shrugged and sipped her foamy latte, her milk mustache framing her purple lipstick. "You'll have to ask the Unit A director. Your old ID, please?" She impatiently wiggled her hand.

Mystified, Macy removed her Unit C security ID from its lanyard and took a shaky breath as she handed it to Purple Fingernails.

"I'll tell you why, honey," said Victoria, breezing over to Macy. "When I told DeMello what you did yesterday, he thought we should reward your gutsy action. He was happy we got it on camera and said we might use it in the last cut. Welcome to the 'A' List."

Before Macy could respond, Victoria linked her arm in a motherly manner and urged her along. "You are now a featured extra. Come with me to wardrobe."

Stunned, Macy followed her through the double doors down a long hallway that opened into a whirlwind of activity. This is what she'd always envisioned a major studio to be like: crew members rushing between sets, pushing carts full of props, and individual rooms with movie star names on the doors.

Now, here she was.

Victoria stopped at the door marked 'Extras' and beamed at Macy.

"Here you go. Julie will get you squared away." Victoria lifted Macy's chin and leaned back. "You're a cute little thing, aren't you?

I can see why our little Nicky likes you." She winked before clicking away in her stilettos.

Macy shook her head in disbelief as she opened the door to yet another flurry of activity inside the Extras dressing room.

"Hey, Applegate, about time you showed up! Congrats on getting into Unit A!" Julie called out from across the room. "Hurry and dress. They're already calling for extras on set."

Macy stood befuddled. "This is way cool... but I don't know what my role is. What am I supposed to do? Am I still a reporter?"

Julie shrugged. "Nick will let you know."

"Nick as in Westwood? Why him?" Macy's face fell. "Where's Sylvia?"

"She had a family emergency in Los Angeles. Nick is filling in for her."

Macy groaned. "But he's the assistant director. Why would he do that?"

"Because DeMello told him to," said Julie. "Come on, hurry!"

"So, I have to work directly with Westwood?" Her voice rose in alarm.

"You worry too much. Most women would die for the chance," admonished Julie, tossing her a pair of shoes. "Get these on quick."

"Julie, what did Westwood say about yesterday? He said he got me out of the pond and warmed me up in his car, but I remember nothing."

"Uh—he didn't explain?" Julie hesitated. "He told me he got you out, warmed you up, then the ambulance came." She took two hangers from the clothes rack and thrust a skirt and blouse at Macy. "Hurry, get these on."

"But how long was he at the hospital?" Macy persisted.

EVERYBODY LOVES POLAR BEARS

"Until you woke up—a couple of hours, maybe? He stopped by to check on you. I waited with him until I knew you were okay, then I had to come back here to work on some stuff for today." Julie fussed with a skirt hem. "How are you feeling?"

"Like I swallowed Cook Inlet."

"What a hoser that you fell into that pond. At least you don't look like *Blue Man Group* today."

"Aw, you're so sweet." Macy flashed a fake smile to her bestie.

She was still wrapping her brain around the fact that Westwood had spent time at the hospital, concerned about her welfare. But then he probably had to make sure she was all right for legal reasons.

"Westwood didn't mention what happened after dip-netting me like a king salmon. Just said he put me in his car to warm me up. What did he tell you?"

"Why don't you ask him?" deflected Julie with a slight shrug.

"What's the big deal? You know something, don't you?" she challenged. "Come on, tell me!"

Julie looked at her warily. "Okay, I'll tell you, but don't get upset."

"Why would I get upset?"

Julie placed her hands on her hips. "Nick should be the one to tell you this. It's not really my place, but he told me, and I didn't know if I should say anything—"

"Jules, out with it!" interrupted Macy. "Just tell me already!"

"Okay, but don't get how you get." Her friend closed an eye and squinted at her. "You were hypothermic, so Nick put you in his SUV. He removed your clothes, then his clothes—to warm you up—you know, until the ambulance showed up. That's all I know." She said it fast and threw up her arms.

Macy fixed her with a long, piercing stare, then her gaze shifted to horror at the realization that Nick had stripped them both down to their birthday suits. Her eyes widened as a nuclear explosion went off in her chest.

"Did I hear you correctly? He took off my clothes—and *his* clothes? Like all of them? Was he completely naked? Was I completely naked?" shrieked Macy. "Both of us? Like ALL THE WAY naked?" One hand shot to her boob, and the other covered her crotch.

"Oh, dear God!" she shrieked even louder as reality dawned. "Holy crap!"

Julie grabbed her shoulders. "Get a grip, Mace. You don't remember?"

"No!" insisted Macy. "Just a vague sensation of someone rubbing my back. I didn't know where I was—I thought I was dreaming. Woke up in the hospital wondering how I got there."

She plopped down on the sofa and covered her face. "Holy flipping hell!"

She snapped her head up herky-jerky, like a chicken. "Why didn't Westwood tell me all that in the hospital yesterday? How am I supposed to merrily prance on set and act like nothing happened?"

"You're an *actress*, remember?" said Julie. "Act like nothing happened. You have scenes to film. Hurry and get dressed." Julie heaved her clothes at her.

Macy lowered her jeans when a sudden knock on the door made her jump. It swung open, and to her horror, Westwood filled the doorway.

"I need four extras pronto," he called out, his eyes resting on Macy. "Hey, Applegate, congrats on being promoted to Unit A."

EVERYBODY LOVES POLAR BEARS

He was all business, as if he saw her undressing every day of the week.

Since he'd apparently gotten naked with her, this must be a super casual thing for him now.

Macy's eyes popped out of her head as she virtually slithered under the sofa.

"For crying out loud, Westwood!" hollered Julie. "What did I tell you about barging in here while people are dressing?"

"What's the holdup?" he barked. "Extras should already be out there!"

Mortified, Macy grimaced and covered herself with a frilly 1980s vintage blouse. But then, why bother when he'd already seen her without clothes?

"Do you mind? This is just a little awkward." She shot him a wide-eyed, caribou-in-the-headlights look.

"We need extras on set ASAP," he mumbled, then vanished out the door and closed it firmly behind him.

Macy swore his face had reddened before dashing back out again. As well, it should have.

"What the heck was *that*?" squealed Macy, looking at Julie with exasperation.

Julie shrugged. "He obviously needed extras on set."

"The audacity of that guy. Does he always barge in here like that? He's my flipping boss! He saw me naked *and* in my underwear. That's like me on my day job, standing in my cubicle wearing nothing but bra and panties, and my freaking boss waltzes in to say I'm late for a meeting." Her heart had leaped into her throat, and she struggled to catch her breath.

Macy shot Julie a horrified look as she wriggled into a navy-blue pencil skirt and a white blouse adorned with so many ruffles Prince would have been envious.

"Your day job boss could use some excitement." Julie pushed Macy into a chair in front of a large makeup mirror and teased her auburn locks into a big, eighties-style do. "Besides, Westwood didn't see you completely naked when he warmed you in his car. He only removed your bra."

"*Only?* He said this?" Macy's eyes became two moons as she stared at Julie in the mirror. "Did he say he left my undies on? Oh gawd, I was wearing my granny panties! I was out of laundry and that's all I had—"

Julie cut in. "Relax, he didn't mention your granny panties." She gave Macy an impish smile. "Guess you'll have to ask him for the gory details."

"I had my undies on when I woke up in the hospital. I dreamed someone had taken off my clothes and was poking me." She turned to her bestie, horrified. "That means my movie boss poked me with his dick? Oh, gawd, I can't show my face out there..." Macy's pulse skittered. Her acting reputation had tarnished before it had a chance to grow up and leave the comfortable nest of her resume.

"Macy, look at the big picture," said Julie firmly. "Nick saved you from advanced hypothermia, which could have killed you." Julie patted her shoulder. "Talk to him about it after filming today. It wouldn't hurt to be nice to him for helping you. You might even say thank you."

"I thanked him yesterday. Before I knew we were naked." Macy tried to steady her shaking fingers as she applied her lipstick. "Now, every time he looks at me, I'll picture him naked. And me naked. And him poking his you-know-what against me."

EVERYBODY LOVES POLAR BEARS

"I can think of worse things. Besides, you're both adults, and you wore your granny panties." Julie finished styling Macy's hair and doused it with hairspray.

"I'm sure the granny panties were my cloak and shield." Macy squeezed her eyes closed. "After he dip-netted me like a salmon."

"At least he didn't gut you and toss you into a cooler." Julie's brow lifted. "Westwood was too busy saving your life to have a hard-on, so I highly doubt that's what poked you."

"Gawd, I'm so embarrassed about the whole thing." Macy coughed from Julie's clouds of hairspray.

"I can think of worse things than the assistant director seeing you naked," said Julie in a matter-of-fact voice. "If this were a porno, him seeing you naked would be normal. Everyone is saying what a superhero you are after saving Victoria from an ice bath. She's the one who told DeMello to move you into Unit A."

Macy nodded. "That was nice of her to do. I'll be sure to thank her."

Westwood rapped on the door, hollering the five minutes were up.

"I don't know what I'm supposed to be doing. I don't have a script for today's scenes. I'm *always* prepared!" Macy's heart sped as she frantically reached behind herself to zip her skirt. "It doesn't help I dreamed last night I went on set naked."

Julie laughed. "Enough with the naked, Applegate! Get over yourself and get out there before they replace you."

Macy sprang from the make-up chair and rushed out the door after the other three women.

Julie called after her. "Nick and DeMello will fill you in. Remember to breathe."

"Easier said than done," Macy retorted over her shoulder. She steadied her breathing to regain composure.

Apprehension and anxiety rolled through her as she followed the other extras and Westwood into an office set with desks and chairs. She felt like a polar bear standing on the planet's last ice floe.

After all, this was a movie about polar bears.

Chapter 12

Nick led the extras along the hallway to the trooper headquarters set, beating himself up for his lapse in judgment.

Why didn't I tell Macy what I had to do to warm her up? Now she thinks I'm some kind of pervert.

He tried to focus on the next scene. Instead, he cogitated on what a chicken-shit he was for not telling Macy the whole story. How could he explain to the woman who despised him he'd stripped them both naked, then pressed their bodies together? He'd done it to prevent her from succumbing to hypothermia, but by doing so—he'd blown his chance of building a positive working relationship with Macy.

When he reached the office set, Nick paused. The four extras bunched up in their haste and smacked into each other. He pointed at the first three women.

"You three, come with me." Leaving Macy standing there, he strode to the other end of the office set and seated the extras at desks.

Macy waited while he directed the other women what to do in the next scene. When he finished, she raised her hand.

"Excuse me. May I have a word with you, please, Mr. Westwood?" She pointed to a corner.

Dread twisted his chest. He'd known this was coming, but her timing wasn't good; today's filming was already behind schedule.

"Can't it wait?" he snapped out impatiently.

"Not when nakedness is on the line," she said candidly, drilling her stare into him so hard it pierced his eyeballs.

"Nakedness?" he echoed in a stage whisper. This caught him off guard, and he glanced around, hoping no one had heard. "Alright. Step over here." His stomach did the hula as he steered Macy to a corner for privacy.

"Sorry, but this discussion needs to happen now." Her eyes traveled to his forearm, and her brow furrowed.

"Let's make it quick then." Nick followed her gaze down to the red and black Haida salmon tattoo wrapped around his forearms. It was a distinctive art form of the Tlingit, Haida, and Tsimshian peoples of Southeast Alaska, easily recognized by any Alaskan.

Whoops.

"Brr. Cold in here, isn't it?" Nick pretended to shiver while tugging his sleeves down to cover his forearms. He chided himself for thoughtlessly rolling up his sleeves.

Macy gave him an odd look. "It's cold everywhere this time of year."

"I know what you're going to say. I should've explained things yesterday—" he started.

Macy cut in. "Why didn't you tell me about the minor details at the hospital?"

"Because you weren't in any shape to handle that info yesterday. Can we talk about this later?"

"Look, I really appreciate what you did. But I had to get the details from someone else."

Nick figured that someone else was Julie. "I didn't think it was that big of a deal."

EVERYBODY LOVES POLAR BEARS

"Taking off my clothes was no big deal? Do you know how humiliating it is for me right now after—after—God, Westwood, you saw me naked and for all I know, you could be a serial killer, plus, I'm not even sure I like you!"

How she got all that out in one breath after nearly drowning yesterday mystified him. At least she was honest. He'd give her that. He tried to let the sting of her not liking him slide off his back.

"If it's any consolation, I saw nothing," he said in a low, measured tone. "I was busy trying to raise your core temperature, so you wouldn't... you know, die."

"Thank you for that, sincerely. But I want to know what you did in the car. Details, please."

He shook his head. "Not now. We're running behind schedule." He shifted impatiently. "Cripes, I mean seriously—you're turning an ant hill into Mount Denali."

"For the love of God. Just tell me!" Her voice rose in pitch and volume, drawing inquisitive glances from others on the set.

Nick shifted his weight to the other foot, blowing out air. "All right. I stopped by to see how filming was going. When you did your Olympic dive, I got you out with a dip net. The water was too cold to dive in and rescue you, or we would've had two drownings." He shrugged.

"You basically dip-netted me like a salmon." She forced a partial smile. "I'm surprised you didn't bonk me on the head and gut me," she quipped. "What makes me curious is how some random L.A. person would even know what a dip net is."

Nick was the one feeling gutted, like he'd done something wrong. He folded his arms in a defensive posture. "You were hypothermic when I fished you from the water, so I put you in my car to warm you up. I did what anyone would have done in that situation—removed your clothes and warmed you with my body temperature."

"Did you remove my—you know—intimates?" She spit it out like it pained her to say it.

He lifted his arms and dropped them. "Why is that such a big deal? I would think you'd be happy that I helped you out. As an Alaskan, surely you can appreciate that." He pointed at her. "I left your panties on, by the way."

"And you deserve a congressional medal of honor for that? Thank God my core temperature *down there* wasn't in any danger." She squeezed her eyes shut. "You should have bonked me on the head and gutted me. I'm so freaking embarrassed."

"If it makes you feel any better, we weren't completely naked." He did his best to dismiss her concern. "Really, there's nothing to be embarrassed about. These things happen. Besides, everything turned out okay."

"I'm sorry. I'm acting like a paranoid weirdo." She squeezed the bridge of her nose.

"Yes, you are." He would not lie to her. "Honestly, there's nothing to be embarrassed about. Let's just move on, okay? We have a movie to film."

"Thanks for helping me. I really do appreciate what you did."

"I was happy to do it."

"I'll *bet* you were," she deadpanned.

"Hey, I'm not a sexual deviant!" he protested. "Serial killer, maybe. But not a sexual deviant." His attempt at humor didn't appear to be working, judging by the thundercloud on her face.

They locked stares, the tension between them boiling like Mount Augustine, ready to erupt and spew hot lava all over the place.

EVERYBODY LOVES POLAR BEARS

"Just wish you would have told me right away, Mr. Westwood."

"I know you don't like me, but I told you before—call me Nick—considering we've been naked together." He couldn't resist that little barb. "Are we done here?"

DeMello shouted from his director's perch on the other side of the set. "Westwood, get this show on the road! Ka-ching, ka-ching, we have work to do."

Welcoming the interruption, Nick raised his forefinger in acknowledgment. He turned back to Macy. "Have I clarified things enough for you?"

"Crystal, *Nick*." Her tone was like an axe splitting firewood.

Geez, what's her problem?

"I guess we're good then. Now if you'll excuse me." He left her gaping after him as he strode over to talk to DeMello.

Nick sensed her eyes boring into his back as he walked away. What did he care about what she thought? He allowed no woman to get under his skin. So why was he letting this one rattle him?

Squaring his shoulders, he compartmentalized himself into director mode. Because this was his main reason for being here.

Not for any other reason. And certainly not because of a woman.

Chapter 13

Macy trudged back to the extras room after filming wrapped for the day, kicking herself for obsessing about nudity rather than appreciating what Nick had done to save her life.

He must think I'm narcissistic and ungrateful. And I told him I didn't like him after what he did? He decides what I do in this movie. Who tells their boss they don't like them? Gawd, I'm an idiot.

She made a sour face as she mentally flogged herself. All right, fine. She'd force herself to be nicer to him from now on. If she wanted more camera time in this movie, she'd better get along with the guy. Talk about getting off on the wrong foot.

Macy changed into her street clothes, grabbed her large bag, and bundled up to head to her car. When she stepped onto the elevator, she stopped herself from groaning out loud to find Westwood talking on his cell. She hesitated, considering whether to bolt back out and take the stairs.

Her feet didn't move, so she sucked it up and dipped her chin in a polite greeting. Her eyes locked onto the floor panel above the door as it closed. They were the only two on the elevator, and a machete couldn't have sliced the tension. Macy sensed his gaze on her as he barked orders into his cell for tomorrow's filming.

When his call ended, the tension mounted. Macy couldn't stand the ear-splitting silence that followed.

EVERYBODY LOVES POLAR BEARS

"Sorry about earlier," she burst out, twisting around to meet his guarded expression. "I acted like an ungrateful jerk. I was overwhelmed by what happened."

"I get that. I'm the one who is sorry." He dropped his cell into his shirt pocket. "I shouldn't have left out those details. I apologize for the distress it caused you."

"I'm not distressed. It's just that..." Macy trailed off. "It was a lot to process. I felt bad for screwing up the scene, and you had to get me out of the pond and...then did what you did."

"Nothing to feel bad about. Can we please forget what happened and start over with a clean slate?" He pantomimed a clapboard with his hands. "New scene. Roll 'em."

Macy appreciated his humor. She swiped her hands together as if wiping off dirt, then displayed both sides to him like a poker dealer. "New slate. New deck of cards. Your deal."

The elevator reached the ground floor, and they both stepped into the foyer of the office building and moved outside. Macy stopped on the sidewalk, watching snowflakes zigzag down, like each one chose where to land. They stood together, letting the silence bounce between them.

Nick didn't appear to be in a hurry to leave. "I feel like I keep having to say this. But the whole naked-in-the-car thing was strictly about helping you. Nothing more." His sincerity drew Macy's gaze.

A corner of her mouth turned up. "Hey, we're starting over, remember?"

Right now, he didn't seem like an assistant movie director. Just a hot-looking guy standing next to her on a snowy evening, who may or may not be a jerk. The jury was still out on that one.

"All right but let me make it up to you. Are you up for a bite to eat?" he asked. "We Angelenos don't know our way around Anchorage. I was hoping you'd have a suggestion."

Macy considered. Maybe this was a way to bridge the gap between them... mend fences and restore equilibrium since they'd be working together.

"You like sushi? I know where they make the best sushi on the West Coast. I'd put it up against anything you have in L.A."

"Lead the way in your car, and I'll follow in mine." He made a grand gesture with his arm while a snowflake rested on his eyelash.

"It's in Muldoon, on the east side. Give me your phone."

He gave it to her, and she tapped his maps app, typed in the sushi restaurant, and handed it back to him. "In case you get lost."

"Thanks, mom. And I won't talk to strangers."

"See that you don't," she joked in a motherly voice. A sense of relief moved through her as the tension between them melted like frost on a warm windshield. "Here's some movie trivia. Remember *The Frozen Ground* film about the serial killer? The real-life serial killer had a bakery in Muldoon. We'll drive right past it."

"Yeah, we used to drive past it when—" he stopped. "What I meant was, I've driven past it. You just made the hair on my neck stand up."

Macy climbed into her Highlander and waited for Nick to get into his car and turn on the headlights. She blinked hers at him, then pulled out as he followed.

When they each pulled into the parking lot of the A-frame sushi restaurant in Muldoon, they parked side by side. Macy led Nick inside, where the hostess set them up in a cozy booth. It was odd to be with him away from the film office and movie sets. And frozen ponds.

EVERYBODY LOVES POLAR BEARS

"How did you wind up in the film industry?" asked Macy, as she settled onto the leather seat.

"Just something I've always wanted to do." He sat back, the dim lighting making him look hotter than Dylan Ford.

Macy flicked her eyes up at the server, who set glasses of water in front of them. "I'll have the bento box with the dragon-roll sushi, please."

"I'll have the same," Nick intoned, his eyes sparkling in the low light.

"I used to mess around with photography and making videos for friends. Did a few weddings and family reunions. Discovered I had a knack for it. Met DeMello at a film festival in Austin, and he hired me as the set photographer for his next movie. I helped the script supervisor with continuity—you know, making sure when we picked up where we left off that things didn't change in the same scenes."

"You mean so the main characters didn't show up in red when they wore blue the day before?"

"Exactly. You'd be surprised how minor details can slip through if you aren't on top of it. Not just with costumes, but other things. One time we filmed a scene for *Terminal Blast* with a family eating spaghetti. The next day, the actors had hamburgers and French fries on their plates in the same scene. Audiences love pointing out those inconsistencies in their reviews. Luckily, I caught that one in time."

"That's great that DeMello mentored you like that. But how did you make the jump from photographer to assistant director?"

"DeMello observed me working with the crew, and he liked how I got along with people. I've done several productions with him. Each time, he's increased my responsibilities. During filming for *Terminal Blast*, I filled in for the assistant director who got covid and had to drop out. Then DeMello offered me the A.D. job for *Everybody Loves Polar Bears,* and here I am." He leaned back as food appeared on the table. "How about you?"

"As you remember from my resume—or maybe you don't—I've done lots of community theater productions. I've had fun doing them, but don't get me started on my recurring nightmares about going onstage without my clothes on." Macy covered her mouth as heat crawled up her neck. "Whoops, sorry about the no clothes comment—that seems to be a theme with us."

Nick laughed infectiously. "You're right about that."

She enjoyed his company more than she'd expected. As their conversation flowed, Macy admitted to herself how down-to-earth Nick really was. He seemed to be on the same wavelength when she talked about her life in Alaska, almost as if he lived here, too.

As they savored their meal, Macy noticed Nick's guarded expression was gone. It was as if they'd stepped inside a bubble where the outside world didn't exist.

They shared common interests, from obscure movie references to downhill skiing. Nick confessed he'd been to Alaska before. He explained his family used to vacation on the Kenai Peninsula. Seeing this side of Nick Westwood was refreshing, and Macy felt more at ease with him.

After a satisfying dinner, they bundled up and headed out to the parking lot, walking side by side. Macy kept her mouth and nose covered to protect her still-sensitive lungs from the frosty night air. The snow had let up, leaving behind a clean, peaceful stillness.

Macy's heart skipped when Nick turned to face her, his eyes fastened to hers. "You're right, the sushi was delicious. I liked the crunchy dragon roll. And thanks... for allowing me to make things right."

Macy fidgeted. While she was more comfortable with him, she was still nervous. "I enjoyed this. See, I can be a good team player."

Nick chuckled. "I have no doubt. I think we'll make a good team on set."

"I never played sports. I learned teamwork by doing stage plays. It was an excellent training ground." Macy took a deep breath, gathering her courage to dine on some crow.

"Nick, when I said I didn't like you earlier, I didn't mean it. It's just that... I wasn't sure how to handle what you did for me."

Nick's expression softened. "Well, thanks for that."

Nervousness twittered her chest. "I don't want my insecurities to prevent me from making a name in the movie business."

"Don't worry, your star will rise. Before you know it, you'll be on the cover of *Celebrity Magazine*." He glanced at his phone. "I have to go. See you tomorrow. Sleep fast."

She drew back in surprise. "My artistic director from the Anchorage Community Theater used to say that at the end of every rehearsal."

"Is that right? Well then, see you tomorrow. Good night." He gave her a hurried wave and headed to his car.

As Macy drove to her condo, she watched neon green lights dance in the sky over the Chugach Range. She slowed, admiring the swirling spectacle, like colorful piano keys playing.

Maybe she and Nick could get along after all. A peace treaty had been initiated, and Macy was glad she'd been receptive to forging one. She resolved to move on after the shaky start to what she hoped might become a film career—one where she'd prove herself as a film actress—and shake off mistakes from her past.

LOLO PAIGE

Macy was glad for the break in the wall with Nick Westwood. She hoped things would go smoothly between them from now on.

Tonight was a good start.

Chapter 14

The next morning, Nick announced they'd be filming at a new location.

"This will be an indoor wedding scene with Dylan and Victoria's characters after they fell in love working to save the polar bears," he informed the cast.

With strategically placed shoulder pads, form-fitting jackets over puffy blouses, and bows that covered their hairdos, Julie had transformed the extras into a retro-1980s wedding extravaganza.

This decade, with its sometimes contradictory and over-the-top style, fascinated Nick. He'd often wondered what life was like back then, without cell phones or computers.

He especially loved the music and had grown up watching MTV with iconic performances by Prince, Michael Jackson, Madonna, and the Talking Heads... artists and groups whose music was as familiar as that of his own generation. All of it was before his time, but he was just as fascinated.

Once the extras were loaded onto buses, they drove to a quaint white church, complete with a picturesque steeple in the Bootlegger's Cove neighborhood west of downtown Anchorage.

Nick watched the extras fill the dark wood pews inside the beautifully decorated church. The crew already had film equipment, lights, and cameras set up in the front and back of the church, but the overcast day reduced the light coming through the rectangular stained-glass windows.

Macy entered the set, her pink satin dress hugging every blessed curve and showing off her generous cleavage. Nick was drawn to the rise and fall of her breasts, like a compass needle to Magnetic North.

He couldn't help but think back to when he'd warmed her inside his SUV. While his focus was keeping Macy alive, it struck him that he'd pressed his bare chest against those beautiful breasts tucked inside that dress. The slight movement below his belt reminded him of that fact, but he couldn't afford his little buddy standing up and saluting right now. Not in a damn church, for cripes' sakes.

Guilt waved through him. He'd fought his impulses that day in the SUV, but he'd peeked—*like when you're a kid and told not to read porn, and you sneaked a peek, anyway.*

Nick beckoned Macy to the front. "You're a friend of the bride, so sit on this side with the bride's family." He motioned her toward the pews left of the center aisle.

He would have liked to sit with her and chat a bit, but he had a scene to direct. Instead, he settled for stealing glances at her. Julie's make-up artists had outdone themselves. Macy was gorgeous in her movie make-up. Then again, they had a pretty face to work with.

Her mouth curled up when she caught him ogling her, and it made his heart stutter. He snapped his gaze to the other actors.

"Last call for places," Nick spoke into his crew mic. "Stand by, get ready to roll," he called out to the camera operator.

Victoria stood at the back of the church, waiting for her cue. She reminded Nick of a vestal virgin, all decked out in glimmering white, like a disco she-ghost. He suppressed a laugh, knowing in real life she'd be wearing Scarlett O'Hara red as a blushing bride.

EVERYBODY LOVES POLAR BEARS

Nick stood at the front of the center aisle, hands on his hips, talking with lights and camera when Dylan swaggered up and assumed the groom's position in his 1980s gray tux, a black and white ascot at his throat. Gasps erupted from the women as he stood smiling at the front of the church full of actors.

Nick rolled his eyes at the movie star's vanity. He positioned his mouthpiece and spoke to the crew wrangling Victoria. "Is Bridezilla ready?"

An exasperated woman's voice crackled in his earpiece. "Bridezilla is on deck, driving us insane. Get her out of here, Westwood. She's obsessing like a real bride."

Nick stifled a laugh, knowing what a capricious perfectionist Victoria could be. "Grip, gaffer, sound mixer, cue up. Alright, rolling! Background, go. Actors go," he called out. "Marker!"

A woman in black extended a slate board, lifted the clapper, and snapped it closed. "Scene forty. Take one."

"Action!" Nick called out.

People rustled and coughed, as they would before a real wedding. Good, that added reality. Everyone was doing what they were supposed to. So far, so good.

Nick's stomach growled. He hadn't eaten since last night's sushi dinner. He'd slept like a hibernating grizzly until his phone alarm woke him this morning.

DeMello slid up beside him. "Thanks for taking care of that close-call situation at Polar Pond. I'm glad you were there. Zippo should have been on top of that. The last thing we want is to drown our local talent. Not good for P.R. Know what I mean?"

"It wasn't Zippo's fault. It was an accident. Applegate prevented Vicky from going in," Nick whispered as Victoria reached the altar.

DeMello patted his arm. "Think Applegate will sue for damages?"

Nick shook his head. "Macy isn't the type. Don't ask me how I know that. I just do." Nick's brow furrowed as he trained his eyes on the actors. "She'll be less likely to sue if you cover her medical costs and compensate her. And a sincere apology for what happened wouldn't hurt. She's not covered by the union."

"Right. I'll do that. Take care of it." DeMello slapped Nick's shoulder. "You're a good man. You know how to cover my ass. That's why you're the brains of this outfit. Make sure we keep Applegate happy. Even if she isn't in the union, if they find out about the incident, an investigation will ensue. I can't afford to have this production shut down. Get what I'm saying?"

"As always. Yes. I've got this." Nick was used to DeMello expecting him to clean things up. He thought about adding another rolling credit in addition to the assistant director: production cleaner. He thought of *Pulp Fiction*. That was a different kind of cleaner.

"All right, then. We're all good. Let's roll it." DeMello twirled his forefinger.

Nick stepped to the side, off camera, and adjusted his headset. He spoke into the mouthpiece. "Cue Victoria."

The elegant movie star glided down the aisle in her white form-fitting dress with its extra-long train, pretending to love the groom, who pretended to love her back. Nick knew they weren't genuinely fond of each other, but they were consummate professionals who got along for the sake of the film. And that's all he cared about.

When the wedding scene ended, DeMello hollered, "Cut! Excellent job, everyone!" He turned back to Nick. "You're doing such a great job. I think I'll have you direct the reception scene." DeMello slapped him on the back with a jovial grin.

"Only if you give me an on-screen credit for assistant director." Nick liked DeMello giving him more responsibility, but he hoped his boss wasn't sneaking off the wagon to go have a brew, as he'd surreptitiously done in the past.

"You got it, buddy," said DeMello as he hurried off.

Nick had covered DeMello's butt by pulling him out of hot water more than once. Last time, when DeMello had seduced a girl he later found out was a minor, Nick had moved swiftly to put out that brush fire. By law, he'd had to inform the girl's parents, which he had—and offered them a substantial sum for their silence and to keep it out of court. Nick had felt like pond scum doing it, but DeMello was his mentor, and he didn't want to screw up their relationship.

"Cast and crew!" Nick called out. "We have to do another take for this scene. Victoria and Dylan's faces were in shadow. We must fix the lighting."

Victoria made a distressed face. "I need to hit the ladies' room."

She glanced up at Zippo, whose eyes had been fixated on her bulbous cleavage. "Honey, there's nothing in here for you."

Zippo blushed, jerked himself upright, and headed off the set. "Light design! We have work to do."

Victoria turned to Nick. "When you have to go, you *have* to go!"

Nick let out a sigh. "We need to fix the lighting and film this scene again."

"No can do right now. Get me a stand-in. The union says I can have a stand-in for technical stuff." Victoria glanced around, spotted Macy, and waggled a finger at her. "Use Bear Woman. Come up here, honey."

Macy mouthed, "Who, me?"

"Who else, baby doll? Get your little derriere up here," ordered Victoria, snapping her fingers and pointing at her mark on the altar. Anyone who didn't know any better would think Victoria was directing.

Macy rose and made her way to where Victoria stood on the altar.

"Thanks, hon. Here's your stand-in, Nick!" Victoria called out. She patted Macy on the head, tossed back her bridal veil, and marched back up the center aisle.

Nick caught the fast exchange of looks between Victoria and Dylan before she'd swished her way to the back of the church. Dylan abruptly followed.

"Dylan!" hollered Nick. "Where the heck are you going?"

"Men's room!" hollered Dylan, hurrying after Victoria.

"Right," Nick muttered under his breath, suspecting Dylan was aiming to get into Victoria's bridal panties and dashed after her to do just that. Despite not being the best of friends, neither could pass up opportunistic sex.

Zippo appeared next to him. "We need to speed up this re-take or we'll run out of time. Nick, can you stand in for Dylan?" He waggled his finger at Nick. "I'll hold your headset. Take the groom's mark."

"Okay, let's get on with it." Nick tossed Zippo his headset and stood on the small X of glow tape on the altar.

Zippo motioned to Macy. "Take your mark on the glow tape next to Nick. We'll go through the motions of the ceremony. Don't worry about the lines, just the blocking."

EVERYBODY LOVES POLAR BEARS

Macy and Nick stood side by side, facing the altar, while the lighting crew made the adjustments. Nick caught a whiff of her cologne mingled with a freshly showered flower scent that he slowly inhaled.

The light designer's voice fed them instructions from his elevated platform next to the altar. "Now face each other for the kissing bit so that we can adjust for the close-ups."

Nick turned toward Macy. She froze like a bear in the headlights, and Nick swallowed a laugh at her wide-eyed expression. He enjoyed the bird's-eye view of her decolletage, and it took every ounce of his self-control not to gawp.

"We don't have to kiss for real. I know you'd rather kiss a moose." Nick flashed her a flirtatious smile. "We'll just stand here and tell jokes."

"I bet I can out-joke you." Macy's eyes twinkled. "What do you call a polar bear who sunbathes?"

"I don't know. What?"

"A solar bear," said Macy with a smug look.

"What do you call a polar bear with no teeth?" volleyed Nick.

Macy shook her head.

"A gummy bear."

She guffawed. "Ha! Where do polar bears keep their money?"

Nick grinned. "In snowbanks."

She frowned. "Hey! How'd you know that one?"

"I Googled polar bear jokes last night. The lighting and sound crews have a running bet on who could come up with the funniest jokes."

"That's cheating," she protested.

Zippo stood in the center aisle and snapped his fingers. "Pay attention, Westwood. I still see shadows on their faces," he said to the lighting crew. He pointed at Nick. "Lean in for the kiss so we can get this close-up lighting adjusted."

Nick moved close and gazed into Macy's pools of green. Was that a welcoming look, or was it something else he was reading? What the heck? He took the risk and closed the distance, pressing his lips to hers. If he misread her welcoming cue, then this would earn him a timeout in hell.

To his delight, Macy wasn't an innocent bystander with his kiss. *She's leaning into me and kissing me back.*

Losing himself in the moment, he removed his arms from around her and cupped her cheeks to deepen the kiss. She let out a squeak, and he smiled into her mouth, hoping no one else had heard it.

A cacophony of cheers erupted from the extras and crew. Someone whistled, and whoops and applause broke out. Nick was aware, but he loved the delectable taste and feel of Macy. No way did he want to stop kissing.

And apparently, she didn't either.

"Hello? Actors? Think you can hold that position, say, for another week?" teased Zippo, eliciting laughter. "Aww, isn't that sweet? I think they're having a moment," he stage-whispered to the waiting actors, who laughed even more.

"Okay, lighting is fixed," announced Zippo. "Get Victoria and Dylan back in here for the re-take. Yoo-hoo, Westwood? We're done here, buddy."

"Get a room!" someone hollered, causing Nick to laugh and break the kiss.

"Had to make sure the lighting was right." Nick's comical expression triggered more laughter.

EVERYBODY LOVES POLAR BEARS

Macy's face turned pink, and she covered her mouth. Her eyes bugged out like she'd been caught stealing candy.

Nick's two-sizes-too-small heart turned to goo and puddled. It impressed him that Macy had allowed herself to be in the moment. He wondered whether she did it to show off her acting skills or if she was truly sincere about it.

Who cares? He loved it either way.

Chapter 15

When Nick lifted his lips from hers, Macy fought to regain control of her senses. She'd kissed him back like an unstoppable bore tide plowing through Turnagain Arm. When he'd deepened the kiss, her body had tumbled into an uncontrollable heap of lust. Only problem was, their panty-melting kiss had been on display out here in front of God, the Jesus, Joseph, and Mary statues, and everyone in the whole flipping production.

Macy was numb with shock when Nick drew back and delivered a funny one-liner. She was relieved when everyone cheered and laughed and hoped no one thought anything of it. She reminded herself stand-ins were supposed to act the same as the main characters in a scene.

As she worked to steady her unruly heartbeat, Macy knew she hadn't been acting when she kissed Nick Westwood. Not by a long shot. She was pretty sure he hadn't been acting either, unless he'd perfected the art of fake kissing along with his multitude of other talents.

"We have another scene to do," said Nick, reverting to director mode. He flashed her a subtle wink. "Way to break a leg on the acting."

"Right. The acting. See you in the next scene." She was tongue-tied after levitating up to the moon and back. Was it wrong to feel lust while standing at a church altar? Maybe it was the romanticism of being in this movie—or the fairy-tale ambiance of the wedding scene—whatever it was, Nick's kiss had her reeling and second-guessing herself.

So much for disliking Nick Westwood.

This was an unforeseen plot twist—despite the fact no cameras were rolling.

After finishing the second take of the church wedding scene, Nick directed everyone upstairs to the church hall to film the reception. He stood in the center of the large room wearing his headset, talking in muted tones into the mouthpiece. When he finished, everyone stood waiting, ready to do the scene.

"Extras, be ready to receive the wedding couple as they enter the reception. Those with cameras, take photos," instructed Nick from the center of the room. "Ozzie will distribute the props."

Ozzie reminded her of a weathered hippie with his long, scraggly ponytail. He puttered along the line of extras, his gray mustache twitching, as he handed out props to the extras. He handed Macy a pocket Instamatic camera used in the eighties, like the one her mom bought from Longs Drugs in Anchorage years ago.

An older woman next to Macy squealed at the orange Kodak disposable camera Ozzie had given her. "I haven't seen one of these in years!" She looked at it from every angle as if she were inspecting a woolly mammoth bone.

Macy turned her vintage camera over, fiddling with it. It was the size of a small wallet, and twice as thick as a modern-day cell phone.

"Okay, everyone, let's get organized. Zippo has told you your marks. Background, action! Vicky and Dylan, action!" called out Nick.

Victoria and Dylan appeared in the double doorway with flushed faces. Macy held the camera at arm's length, the same way she'd position a smart phone. The Instamatic felt strange in her grip, and she strained to see Victoria and Dylan in the impossibly tiny square window.

"Cut!" yelled Westwood. "Miss Applegate, that's not how we held cameras in the eighties."

Macy heaved out a sigh at having messed up another scene. At least there was no icy pond threatening to end her life this time.

Nick strode over to her with his amiable smile, her pulse ticking up as he stopped in front of her. He plucked the camera from her fingers in a lighthearted manner.

"Hold the camera next to your eye and look through the viewfinder. There were no cell phones back then, so don't hold it like one." He showed her, as if teaching a photography class.

"Got it." Macy took the camera and fumbled with it, discombobulated by Nick's proximity.

The unexpected kiss during the stand-in scene had flipped a swoony switch inside of her. Since then, she'd been in a perpetual state of discombobulation, despite her resolve to dislike Nick Westwood. Then again, maybe what she was feeling was only her imagination. After all, they'd been acting, right?

As filming progressed for the faux wedding reception, Macy noticed Nick darting glances in her direction. She wondered if anyone else had noticed their tectonic shift. Probably not. The other actors were preoccupied with getting as much on-camera time as possible, and the crew only focused on the filming.

For the next take, Nick selected a group of women to catch the bridal bouquet. He motioned his head at Macy to stand front and center. It thrilled her that Nick was giving her more camera time.

EVERYBODY LOVES POLAR BEARS

"I heard about that kiss," Victoria whispered in her ear with a cat-eyed look as she brushed past Macy. "Get your catcher's mitt ready. It's coming straight to home plate." Victoria positioned herself to toss the bouquet, winking at Macy.

"Ladies, act like you want that bouquet more than anything you've ever wanted in your life!" directed Nick. "Everyone else, join in the fun. Come on, get good and rowdy."

Wedding guests whooped and hollered as Macy braced herself and planted her feet apart, like a shortstop expecting an easy out. Her peripheral vision caught Nick watching closely as she raised her arms over her head.

"Action!" Nick called out, standing off to the side with folded arms.

Victoria delivered her line. "Get ready, ladies! Here it comes!" She turned her back and tossed it high over the back of her head.

The bouquet flew into the air, and Macy tracked it expertly, her eyes never leaving the descending flowers. She homed in on the bouquet as it rose and plummeted into the multitude of outstretched hands. She prepared to catch it when a taller woman snapped out a long arm and snatched the falling bouquet.

"Dammit!" yelled Macy, beside herself. "I'm supposed to catch that!"

"Fight for it, ladies!" Nick yelled amid the crowd noise. "Give us some action!"

"I'll give you action, all right." Macy didn't hesitate. Determined, she tackled the woman, who doubled over the bouquet and clutched it to her stomach like grim death. Both women tumbled to the floor, tussling.

The crowd closed in on the two brawling women, rolling around like a couple of contenders in a women's professional wrestling match.

"Let go!" Macy gritted her teeth as she grappled for the handle. Something ripped when she yanked the bouquet from the woman's grasp and raised it in triumph, like an Olympic torch. The crowd of actors erupted with laughter and cheers.

The woman cussed, but Macy couldn't hear what she said amid the crowd noise. She didn't know whether cameras were still rolling, but she assumed they were. She did her level best to act like a lucky recipient next in line for the bridal throne. Victorious, she pushed to her feet, still holding the mangled bouquet high.

"Cut!" hollered Nick, arriving in front of Macy with his eyeballs locked onto her chest.

"Whoa, wardrobe malfunction, Cinnamon! Get this woman a pole!" Victoria's boisterous voice dissolved into laughter.

Macy glanced down, horrified. Her dress had torn down the middle, fully exposing her boob. She quickly stuffed the renegade breast inside her pushup bra and held the bouquet over the torn bodice.

To Macy's relief, Nick glossed over the wardrobe malfunction. "That's a wrap, people! Excellent job, everyone. Remember to stick your props in the prop box when you exit the set." He leaned into her. "Nice offensive tackle. You should play for the Rams."

"You said give you some action, so I did." She glanced down at the tattered remains of the bouquet and the collateral damage of silk flowers scattered on the floor.

"We're keeping that take. It spiced things up in the movie. Decent work today." Nick winked, then ambled over to Zippo.

EVERYBODY LOVES POLAR BEARS

"That was quite the barroom brawl," rumbled a deep voice behind her. "You've caught the director's eye. You'll have more screen time from now on."

Macy turned to see the iconic Dylan Ford as she headed toward the coatroom to collect her winter gear for the bus ride back to the movie office. "For exhibiting myself? I didn't do it deliberately."

"Your bouquet takedown was impressive." A gleam of interest sparked Dylan's eyes. "How about dinner with me tonight?"

"Dinner?" Macy stopped in surprise. "Tonight?"

"I have reservations for seven p.m. at the Crow's Nest in the Captain Cook Hotel if you'd care to join me." Dylan flashed the effervescent smile she'd seen online and on countless magazine covers.

First a lunch invitation, now a dinner? She was in such a good mood after today; she thought it would be a fun experience to say she had dinner with a famous movie star. "Sure, why not?"

"Perfect," he quipped as if he'd just clinched a movie deal. "I can send a car for you, or you can meet me there, whichever you prefer."

"I'll drive myself and meet you there. See you then," she called after him as he hurried outside to his waiting limousine.

Macy reminded herself how she didn't want to move up the movie ladder. But what harm was there with one dinner?

None, if I leave after dinner and drive myself home.

Macy's heart raced with a mix of excitement and nerves as she watched Dylan Ford stride out to his limo. It wasn't every day that a world-renowned movie icon asked her to dinner. She reminded herself to keep everything casual and enjoy the evening. It was simply dinner between two coworkers while working on a movie.

Guilt hit her like a moon rock as she wondered what Nick was doing for dinner tonight. That kiss had been out of this world.

But it was only a stand-in kiss. Nothing more.

If she kept telling herself that, maybe she'd believe it. Although she didn't share the same level of admiration for Dylan as countless other fans, she felt it would be rude to turn down a second invitation.

It's only a business dinner. Nothing more.

As Macy gathered her winter gear and prepared to board the bus to the movie office, she embraced this thrilling rollercoaster ride that her life had suddenly become. Today's unanticipated wardrobe malfunction had been a big hit with the cast and crew, but she hoped her bare boob would hit the cutting room floor. It was a family movie, after all.

Maybe that's why Dylan sought her out for a dinner invitation. So what? She'd go anyway. What's the worst that could happen?

I'm the one in charge of my life. I'm the one in control.

With a spring in her step and a heart-load of ambition, Macy headed out the door to get ready for her big evening.

Chapter 16

Macy homed in on Dylan Ford as she strolled through the Crow's Nest on the twentieth floor of the Captain Cook Hotel. A swarm of people surrounded his table, catering to his every need as she approached. He'd chosen the table in her favorite corner, the one that provided breathtaking vistas of the city lights.

She stood across the table from him, her hand on a chair. A server greeted her. "Are you with Mr. Ford?"

"Yes, I am." Macy smiled at the woman. She assumed an air of self-importance as another server pulled out her chair and motioned her to sit. "Thank you." She gave him a polite smile.

"My, aren't you lovely this evening?" Dylan's deep blue gaze gleamed at her over the brandy snifter he brought to his lips. He must be wearing tinted lenses. No one had eyes that blue—except maybe Nick Westwood—not that she'd intentionally noticed, except *his* were like pools of sapphire.

"I took the liberty of ordering you a drink. As an Alaskan, I assume you like that god-awful salmon-flavored vodka?" He beamed his Beverly Hills smile at her.

"Not especially." She preferred her salmon on a plate.

The server placed a Bloody Mary on the table, topped with a skewered salad of celery, olives, and other vegetables. She wasn't a Bloody Mary fan, but she gave him a polite nod.

"Thanks," she said, fiddling with the garnish.

"Tell me about yourself." Dylan casually leaned back, sipping his brandy.

She had to admit that he looked like a hot million in his dark silk suit. Possibly Armani? Someone must have custom-made his jacket, and while she couldn't see his pants, she figured they fit him perfectly.

"I was born and raised in Anchorage, and my day job is with a federal agency that regulates the oil and gas industry in Alaska."

"Oh, is that right?" He regarded her thoughtfully. "So, why are you working on this movie?"

"I've done years of local acting on stage. Wanted to try film acting." She sipped her drink. "It also helps with cabin fever."

"What's that, some kind of disease?"

She laughed at his lower forty-eight naïveté. "No, it's what we say when going bonkers from being cooped up during the long winters."

"Ah." He smoothed the table with a diamond-studded finger, his Rolex glinting from the flickering table candle. "I get cabin fever when it's too hot to go outside in L.A."

Somehow, Macy couldn't relate to that.

A server appeared to take their orders.

"Get whatever you like. The production is paying for this." He turned to the server. "Is your salmon grass fed?"

Macy choked on her celery and flicked her eyes up at the server, who froze with a strange look on his face. "Uh, no, sir. Not unless grass grows in the ocean."

Macy secretly high-fived the guy and grinned at him.

"Ha, I'm just messing with you," teased Dylan. "I'll take the Halibut Olympia."

EVERYBODY LOVES POLAR BEARS

"I'm glad you weren't serious," said Macy. "Most people ask where the igloos and ice worms are, and who mows the tundra."

"I have yet to see the tundra under all this snow." He sipped his brandy.

"You'll have to come back in the summer for that." Macy turned to the server. "I'll have a grilled king salmon steak with a Caesar salad."

"Ah, a healthy eater. I like that," said Dylan, as if evaluating her for a modeling job. "You have a presence that works well on film. You strike me as someone who has 'It.'"

She gave him a blank look. "Meaning what?"

"Have you been told you have a wonderful stage presence?"

"Yes."

"Well, you have an excellent camera presence. You move with grace, have a smooth vocal quality, and use good facial expression. I watched you on set today. I know outstanding talent when I see it." The way he said it warmed her.

"Thank you. I appreciate you saying that."

When the food arrived, they made polite conversation between bites. Macy chuckled to herself. She conversed with Dylan as if she hung out at his poolside digs every day of the week. When they finished eating, Dylan leaned back and ordered an after-dinner drink.

"You know, I have a substantial pull in the film business," he said offhandedly. "I can get you an agent, auditions, whatever you want. Just name it."

"And you would do this because...?" She let it hang there, instinctively knowing what was coming.

"Because I like you. I did from the moment I saw you. I thought you could come back to my room after dinner so we could discuss it."

So, there it was: the dangle of the hook. He'd played it like the smooth roll of a cue ball into a corner pocket. Actors played according to a script, and this guy was no exception. She should know, since she was one.

"Oh, wish I could," she demurred, priding herself on not taking his bait. "But I have obligations at home and have to get going." The words were hardly out of her mouth when a group of young women discovered Dylan and hustled over from the bar.

"Oh my God, it's Dylan Ford!" squealed a silky-haired blonde who spilled over the top of her dress. Her two compadres joined her in a gush fest.

Dylan's attention switched to the three young women swooning over him, wanting selfies and autographs. He didn't blink when Macy quietly rose and ducked out of the restaurant. In fact, he never even noticed.

On her way out, she left some bills with the cashier. "This is for the king salmon and my drink. I don't want you-know-who to pay for it." She winked at the guy, then stepped over to the elevator.

She couldn't help wondering what making love with Dylan Ford would have been like. No doubt, he'd invite the three young women to his hotel room using the same smooth talk he'd attempted on Macy.

She was proud of herself for not giving in to his advances, despite her intense desire for success in the movie industry.

She was determined to earn her own way, as her parents had taught her.

Chapter 17

Nick had finally summoned the nerve to ask Macy to dinner by the time filming had wrapped yesterday. Unfortunately, Dylan beat him to the punch and asked her first. Her easy acceptance of his invitation irritated Nick as he approached the women's dressing room the next morning. He placed his hand on the doorknob, then remembered Julie chewing him out.

He knocked, ever so respectfully.

Julie opened the door a crack. "Good morning, lover boy. I adored that sumptuous lip lock you planted on my roomie yesterday."

Nick narrowed his eyes. "You know darn well that was just stand-in acting."

Julie lifted a brow. "From where I stood, it was more than a routine stand-in."

"That obvious, huh?" Nick wasn't the least bit uncomfortable about it. In fact, he was downright giddy. "Hey, it's the movies. No one takes anything seriously."

"You joked about it, so no one thought anything of it." She winked at him. "But from what I know of you, and knowing my bestie, that kiss was more than movie acting."

Nick glossed over it. "Send the extras to the holding area. We're ready to film."

"Will do." Julie closed the door, and Nick walked down the hall to the spacious holding room, where actors waited to be called on the set.

Macy appeared. "Ready to go," she said breathlessly. She was radiant, and Nick's warped male brain wondered if she had sex with Dylan last night.

"Good morning. Get enough rest last night?" He was fishing, but hopefully Macy wouldn't suspect that he was.

"Slept like a baby." She hunched her shoulders in a happy motion.

"Good to hear it." He wondered if this was an aura of a sexually satisfied woman. He'd weasel the details from Dylan later, which wouldn't be difficult. Dylan loved to brag about his fan conquests.

After the actors had assembled in the waiting area, Nick grouped them in order of their entrance on the set to simulate a busy agency office.

He glanced at the scene sketch he'd roughed out on his clipboard for the starting positions. "Listen up, people. This'll be a long day. If you get hungry, help yourself." He pointed to the long table of delectable foods the caterers had arranged.

"Quick reminder: don't talk to The Talent unless they talk to you first." *Like Dylan Predator Ford,* he thought grimly, glancing at Macy.

She smiled innocently. He didn't want that innocence to be taken advantage of.

As Nick moved on and off the set to retrieve groups of extras to get them situated—he was proud of his wrangling abilities—he did his best not to focus on Macy, but he couldn't help locking onto her like a heat-seeking missile each time he entered the extras' holding room.

EVERYBODY LOVES POLAR BEARS

Like now, for instance.

Male actors gathered around Macy at the snack table like wolves on a kill, talking—or flirting—he was a guy; he knew the difference.

Why can't these guys let her eat in peace?

Nick moseyed up to interrupt their conversation. "Macy, come with me, please."

"Sure," she said with her mouth full, wiping cookie crumbs from her lips. She walked alongside him, chewing as fast as she could to gulp down her cookie. "I'm excited for today."

"Fantastic." Nick hung onto his professional demeanor, hard as it was—they had work to do. He led Macy on the set, over to a map holder along one wall. He lifted four rolled-up maps and gave them to her.

"Your job for this scene is to carry these in when you enter. Place three in the rack and carry one to that desk." He pointed to a vintage oak desk in the center of the set. "Unroll it and spread it out for Dylan. Got it?" He wanted to kiss those gorgeous lips again.

"Got it." She took the maps and sent him a mercurial smile that went straight to his man parts.

Down, boy. Don't need a boner on set today.

"Return to the extras holding room until I call Background," he ordered.

Macy did as he instructed. Nick wished all actors would do his bidding so readily. He liked that Macy was a team player. What a joy if all his actors would play together and get along in the sandbox. Dream on, he told himself.

When Nick completed the blocking for the remaining groups, he strolled back to the extras room and couldn't believe what he saw. Then again, it didn't surprise him.

Dylan Ford was face down on the floor, doing one-armed pushups next to the women lined up in their chairs. Clearly showing off for the ladies. Wardrobe would freak, seeing him doing this in his brown vintage suit. With his slick-backed dark hair, Dylan resembled a mobster rather than the politician role he played. *A much better fit,* thought Nick.

"Hey, Macy!"

Nick snapped his head to see Andrew, Macy's friend, waving at her from across the room. He lifted his cell phone to capture a photo of Dylan doing his show-off antics, oblivious to Nick's presence.

Does Andrew think I'll look the other way?

Nick glanced at Macy's horrified expression as she swiped her forefinger across her throat in a *stop* motion to Andrew, then pointed at Nick, who was aghast at the dumb gutsy move. Nick furrowed his brow, not wanting to call Andrew out for it, but as the assistant director and extras wrangler, he had no choice.

Rules were rules. Nick's chest clenched as he strode over to Andrew and held out his hand. "Give it up, dude."

Andrew gave him the cell phone, and Nick tapped it. "Dammit!" he said, shaking his head. This bonehead had taken a ton of on-set photos, and some had already shown up on social media. Nick deleted every photo, returned the phone, and pointed to the door.

"You violated your NDA. You're done, bro. Collect your pay on the way out."

Andrew appeared crestfallen as he skulked toward the exit. The door slammed shut behind him, and all the actors focused on Nick in the stunned silence that followed.

EVERYBODY LOVES POLAR BEARS

"What did he think would happen?" muttered one of the male extras.

Macy fixed a firm look on Nick. "Wasn't that a tad harsh?"

"We informed everyone about the no cell phones policy the first day at the production meeting. We also remind everyone in our daily announcements and in every email. Sorry, but those are the rules." His take-no-prisoner's tone reverberated around the room.

The air was heavy with anticipation as all eyes fixed on Nick and Macy, waiting to see what would happen next. Most of the extras had seen their marathon stand-in kiss the day before and were no doubt expecting intense drama.

"It's go time!" DeMello's voice rang out, interrupting the tension. "Westwood, wrangle the extras. Pronto!"

Nick breathed a sigh of thanks for the interruption. He didn't enjoy playing the heavy.

"Places!" he called out. "All actors, take your starting positions for the next scene." He paused while everyone scurried into position. "Everyone ready? Background, go! Actors, go! Roll tape." Although rolling tape was outdated in this digital environment, he still liked the sound of it.

The extras entered the set in the precise order Nick had directed. Macy played Victoria's friend, who also worked in this office. As she set the map on the desk per Nick's instructions, it snapped back with an eerie force, as if a ghostly presence insisted that it stay closed.

Different movie.

Macy wrestled with the stubborn thing, and Nick stifled a laugh. Dylan shifted impatiently while Macy fought with it. This reminded him of the hilarious antics he'd seen in old Carol Burnett episodes.

"Cut!" yelled DeMello. "Westwood, get the map thing figured out."

Nick grabbed two empty coffee mugs and strode on set. "Macy, use these." He unrolled the map and set a mug in both upper corners, then slid his palms to the two lower ones. "Easy peasy, see?"

Macy bristled, clearly taking offense. "I could have figured that out on my own," she said icily.

What is her freaking problem? One minute she likes me; the next minute she turns on me like a mama grizzly.

"Quick problem-solving is the name of the game today," he said brusquely. "Places again, people. Ready? Roll it." He twirled his forefinger.

The clapperboard woman dashed out and snapped the board to document the second take.

DeMello yelled, "Action!"

Macy once again stashed her maps and headed to the desk. This time, she tripped and flopped onto the desk like a drunken seal. "Ugh!"

"Cut! What the devil was *that?*" yelled DeMello.

"I'm sorry." Macy returned to her mark and positioned herself for a third take.

Nick sensed she wasn't having a good day, and he suspected why.

Maybe she's pissed at me for firing her friend Andrew.

He couldn't figure why else she'd be giving him the cold shoulder.

EVERYBODY LOVES POLAR BEARS

"Action!" Macy strode out with the other extras once again and did her part. This time, she smoothly situated the map.

"That's it," said Nick under his breath.

Dylan moved close to Macy, pressing against her hind end while he peered over her shoulder at the map. Anger rose in Nick like a Cook Inlet tide. He couldn't stop thinking about what happened between them on their dinner date. His mind went straight to the gutter.

Dylan delivered his line. "The Chack-chee Sea is where the polar bears are trapped on the melting ice floes."

Macy swiveled her head toward him. "It's pronounced 'Choock-chee,' not 'Chack-chee.' And earlier you said 'Val-dezz.' It's Val-deez."

Nick grimaced. Macy was right. Those were the correct pronunciations.

"Cut!" DeMello's annoyed voice sliced the air. "Will someone please teach these actors how to pronounce Alaskan locations? Westwood, get on this!"

Nick strode onto the set with a solemn look. "First off, do not correct The Talent in the middle of a scene. That's my job," he said to Macy. He turned to Dylan. "It's pronounced 'Choock-chee,' just as she said." He said it with more venom than he intended.

With a raised brow, Dylan shot Nick a disapproving glance, silently conveying his displeasure at Nick's sharp tone.

Nick announced to everyone on the set, "All actors, please check with me before your scenes if you aren't sure how to pronounce these Alaskan names."

Macy and Dylan both scowled at him as they exited for another take.

Macy whispered to Nick as she brushed past. "Why do I have this feeling you didn't grow up in Los Angeles?"

Nick stiffened and ignored her question. He moved to stand next to DeMello—hoping he hadn't let the moose out of the bag. He recalled how Macy had stared at his tattoos when he'd thoughtlessly exposed his forearms. He wondered if she was on a fishing expedition to find out about his guilt-ridden secret.

After nine more takes, everyone was bone tired and short-tempered. When filming wrapped for the day, Nick strode down to the extras' dressing room to find an open door and an empty room.

Macy had gone home without so much as a howdy-doo or a goodbye. Nick figured the best thing to do was head to his hotel, lie low, and get some shuteye.

"Great," he muttered, tugging on his coat and heading outside. "That's all I need is for everyone in L.A. to find out about my background."

Nick trudged through the frigid air to his rental. Unable to find the windshield scraper, he resorted to yanking a credit card from his wallet to scrape away the intricate frost patterns on the glass.

"Why does life have to be so freaking complicated?" he grumbled, knowing full well why.

He'd created this god-awful mess for himself, and now he had to keep others from finding out his secret.

Chapter 18

Macy's phone startled her awake, and she rolled over in the dark, groaning. She nudged an eyelid open. "Who the heck is calling in the middle of the night?"

With a hesitant tap, she accepted the call and brought it close to her ear.

"This is Julie. I'm on set because they called me in early. There's been a sudden change of plans. You're driving up to Talkeetna right away for Unit A filming, so pack your bag and get down here."

It took a moment for this fresh development to arrange itself inside Macy's groggy brain. She ran her fingers along the edge of her phone, squinting at the intrusive glare of her screen as the tiny date came into focus.

"Wait—the Talkeetna location film shoot isn't until several days from now."

"Change of plans. See you when you get here," said Julie, ending the call.

Macy pointed her key fob out the window of her condo and clicked the remote start. When her car blinked back a welcoming hello with its headlights, she raced around gathering necessities and jamming extra warm clothing into her duffel and daypack.

She rushed outside into the clear, brisk morning. The sky was dark except for the neon green Aurora Borealis flirting with the top of the Chugach Range. She sank into the driver's seat and watched the lights dance as they played piano over the mountain tops.

When she pulled into the film office parking lot, Nick was busy loading equipment into the back of a truck. She rolled to a stop and watched him for a minute, noting how easily he bantered with the production crew. His relaxed and cheerful expression was the opposite of her groggy one in the early morning darkness.

Macy climbed out of her car and walked toward him as a chilly Cook Inlet breeze woke up her face.

Nick looked up and brightened. "Good morning, Applegate. I told Julie to call you. Thanks for showing up on such short notice." He glanced at his car, then back at Macy. "Want to ride along with me?"

His invitation surprised her, but she reckoned after being naked with the guy and kissing him, this was an okay thing to do.

She also had burning questions, but figured she'd start with the easy ones. "How long will we be in Talkeetna?"

"Today and tomorrow. We drive back tomorrow night." Nick pointed to the luxury SUV she hadn't remembered inhabiting after her Polar Pond mishap. "Load your gear, then can you please go inside for some coffee and muffins? I would do it, but I must brief the crew on some last-minute items. We'll leave soon as we get all the film equipment loaded onto this truck."

"Will do." Macy noticed the enormous white boots at the end of Nick's slender blue-jeaned legs, like volleyballs glued to his feet. "I've never seen a Californian wear bunny boots."

Nick gave her a quick shrug. "Someone advised that I get a pair at the Army Navy store."

"Right," replied Macy, not believing a word he said. Things weren't adding up with Nick Westwood, and she was curious to find out why.

EVERYBODY LOVES POLAR BEARS

She ran inside to load up on coffee and muffins after tossing her gear into his SUV. Arranging the cardboard coffees in their drink holders on the dash, Macy climbed inside Nick's idling vehicle and settled into the heated passenger seat. She retrieved her phone and typed Nick Westwood into a search engine. She hadn't dug very deep the first time she'd looked him up before her audition.

Up popped Nick's IMDb page with his movie credits and the productions he'd worked on that she'd seen online. She raised her brows at the big names associated with his productions. According to his credits, he'd done everything from script supervisor to transportation coordinator, then assistant director for the past five years.

Macy kept scrolling, noting more movies Nick had worked on. She kept one eye on him as he talked to the production crew, and the other on her phone as she typed his name along with 'Alaska' into the search engine.

Nothing came up other than the local media announcements and *Variety* magazine announcing that he, along with Logan DeMello, would be directing the movie about polar bears on location in Alaska.

Macy frowned as she scrolled further but saw nothing else about Nick Westwood. Then, a light switched on in her brain. She recalled that day in the Alyeska ski lodge when she noted Andreanoff on Nick's credit card.

What the heck? It's worth a try.

She typed it in. Several Andreanoff's appeared, many in Fairbanks, and others in western Alaska and on the Kenai Peninsula. Macy stole a glance at Nick. He gestured while explaining something to Zippo.

Macy scrolled past photos of a basketball team when one caught her eye. A young Nick Westwood stood grinning in the frame as he held a basketball. A Kenai Peninsula newspaper article followed, with a headline dated sixteen years earlier: *Basketball Point Guard Viktor Andreanoff Wins Full Ride Scholarship to UCLA.*

Macy blinked in disbelief. *Viktor Andreanoff?* But wait, Westwood said he was born and raised in Los Angeles. She read with disbelief how Soldotna High School had lauded him after winning game after game. Then the puzzle pieces fell amazingly into place.

"I knew it!" she muttered to her phone. "You were born and raised Alaskan, Nick Westwood! Or should I say, Viktor?" Why did he change his name and claim California as his birthplace? Most people were proud to be from the 49th state.

His real name was of Russian descent. Maybe he wanted to hide that part of his Alaskan heritage. People in the movie business often changed their names for one reason or another.

Macy sped through another article that caught her eye—a newspaper announcement about a planned wedding—for Viktor Andreanoff and Gloria Haverly. A photo of the couple appeared next to it. Westwood was hot, even back then. His girlfriend was also quite pretty.

Wait—did he marry this woman?

Nick opened the driver's side door. Macy came off the seat, her phone sailing from her grip. It landed face up on the floor with Nick and his fiancée's pearly whites beaming up at her.

"Ready to go?" Nick's eyes gleamed as he slid into the driver's seat. "Took forever to load that doggone truck." He glanced over at her. "What's the matter?"

EVERYBODY LOVES POLAR BEARS

"Oh, no, just dropped my phone," she said in a cheerful tone. "Slippery little bugger. Let's see, it's—" Macy bent and snatched her cell, forcing her heart back down after it'd sprung to her throat. She tapped a button to darken the screen. Now that she and Nick were on better terms, she didn't want to mess things up by him finding her digging into his past.

Nick motioned at her phone. "What time is it?"

"Oh, uh, let's see." Macy tilted the phone away from him, tapped her screen, and got rid of the internet photo. She tapped the time icon. "It's 5 a.m."

"We'd better get it in gear. Didn't think loading up would take so long." Nick changed into his athletic shoes and tossed the bunny boots into the back seat. He shifted into gear and pulled onto 6th Avenue, which became the Glenn Highway leading north out of Anchorage.

Macy was dying to read the rest of the engagement article but had only gotten as far as the photo and the wedding headline. She wanted to broach the subject with Nick but didn't know how to do it gracefully. It wasn't exactly a casual topic for discussion.

As Nick drove them out of town with headlights gleaming strips of highway ice, the city lights faded, and Macy focused on the playful Aurora tap-dancing on the peaks of the Chugach Range. Her mind raced after what she'd learned about Nick. She was still trying to process it.

"The lights are beautiful this morning," she commented benignly.

"Spectacular. I watched them in the wee hours." Nick peered north toward the majestic Alaska Range. "Couldn't sleep, so I got up and worked on what we needed for our Talkeetna shoot."

"Why couldn't you sleep?"

"Kept thinking about work." He shook his head. "I want things to go smoothly on this remote shoot. I have a hundred checklists, so I don't forget anything. You know how it is when you work remote up here. Can't exactly run down to a corner store for an extra film camera or a coaxial cable."

"Ha, right," she said knowingly, noticing how Nick seemed to know his way around. Of course, he did—he was born and raised Alaskan. He probably had an *Alaska Grown* t-shirt hidden in the recesses of his closet back in L.A.

When they reached Wasilla, Nick turned onto the Parks Highway. "Glad the weather is behaving, but there are still icy patches. Forgot how dark it is here in the winter." He switched on his brights.

Bingo. Now was the time to bring it up.

"You *forgot* how dark it is, or are you surprised by it?" Macy gazed at him intently.

He gave her a strange look and seemed to check himself. "I'm surprised by it."

"I don't think you're surprised," she ventured. "I think you forgot. First, you warned me about moose on the highway. Then I saw the Haida tattoo on your arm...and the bunny boots." She hesitated. "But the dead giveaway was seeing another name on your credit card at Alyeska."

Silence, while she studied him with bated breath to see how he'd respond. She sensed his wheels spinning as he chewed his lip and peered through the windshield.

Macy made it easier for him. "You're really Viktor Andreanoff from Alaska, aren't you?"

"Ha, guess I'm busted." He slanted her a lopsided grin. "Couldn't sneak one past you, could I?"

EVERYBODY LOVES POLAR BEARS

"So, when did you move to California?"

He shot her a sideways glance. "Five years ago. Before that—"

"You went to UCLA on a full-ride scholarship," she finished for him.

His brows winged up. "You found the *other* me online. Good detective work."

"It wasn't hard once I figured out your real name. Should I call you Vik? Why did you change your name, anyway?"

He shot her a sideways glance. "Having a Russian heritage isn't exactly popular these days."

"I don't see why not, what with emphasis on diversity these days, especially in the film community," she pointed out.

"True, but people have biases. I was born in Alaska, but people assume I'm Russian when they hear my name."

"Most aren't aware of Alaska's Russian heritage," she replied as they whizzed past a moose on the side of the highway. "But why hide it? I would think you'd be proud of it."

"I am proud of it. When I started out in the film business, it was easier to change my name and say I grew up in L.A. It's hard to explain—I found I had more credibility."

"But why hide your Alaskan background? I mean, where does that get you? I would think you'd be proud of it. You seem paranoid for no good reason."

"That isn't it." He shook his head. "You don't understand what it's like starting in the film business when you don't have connections. It's extremely competitive, and credibility is everything. You need every advantage. I have more cred claiming I'm Nick Westwood from Southern California. Trust me on that."

"Your last name seems a play on words of a famous Hollywood icon. Was that deliberate?"

"Yep." He gave her a lopsided grin. "He's my idol and always will be."

She nodded in understanding. "And no one sees through that?"

"No one has brought it up. So far, anyway."

Macy studied the white dashes as they disappeared under the car. "I saw a photo of you online with a woman named Gloria. Were you married?"

"She died in a head-on collision on the Sterling Highway while I was away at school. She'd planned to go to L.A. and move in with me the following week."

Macy chided herself for having judged him so harshly. "I'm so sorry."

He shrugged. "Happened a long time ago. After the accident, I came home to help Gloria's parents deal with her death. Worked on my uncle's fishing charter boat for a few summers in Homer. Then I took a job in L.A. that one of my professors set up for me."

"That must have been terribly difficult," she said softly. "But honestly, you don't need to hide that you're an Alaskan anymore. You've proven yourself in the film industry by racking up a list of impressive film credits."

"Is this the first time you've been back since...?" she trailed off.

"Yep. Alaska is the same as when I left it. Wild and spectacular—and just as dangerous," he added.

"Some things never change. We still do polar plunges up here but mostly for charity." She cleared her throat. "Mine was the exception."

"Just don't go saving any more movie stars." His laugh was warm and rich. She wished she'd known him in his teen years, growing up in Alaska.

EVERYBODY LOVES POLAR BEARS

"Victoria thinks I'm her bear protector. Hey, Viktor and Victoria." She chortled and drew back to scrutinize him. "You don't look like a Viktor to me. Nick suits you much better."

"They called me Vik back home." He gave her a broad smile. "It rhymes with Nick, so was easy to get used to."

"What about all the legal stuff, like your social security number and your driver's license? Does DeMello know?"

"If he does, he hasn't mentioned it. I had a California driver's license by the time he first hired me, so my being from Alaska never came up. I swore his hiring supervisor to secrecy about my name in return for some favors. Hollywood is a favors kind of town." He smirked at the windshield.

"How'd you come up with Nick?"

He sent her a sidelong glance. "Nikolai is my middle name, so I dropped Viktor to go by Nick." He hesitated. "Can I trust you not to say anything?"

"Possibly for five hundred grand," she teased. "Maybe we could work out a deal."

"You drive a hard bargain. How can I be sure you won't divulge my secret?"

"Anchorage is a favors town too. I'll do you this favor for having saved my life." Secretly, it elated her to learn Nick was an Alaskan. She didn't give a flip about his heritage. "Just keep on being Bruce Wayne. Why would I blow your cover, Batman?"

Nick's mouth curved into an irresistibly devastating grin. "Because we were naked together before we really knew each other?"

"Oh, that minor detail. Well, I won't hold it against you." She snuggled down in her seat and closed her eyes, her curiosity satisfied.

Nick pointed his thumb at the back seat. "Lay your seat back and get some shuteye." He tapped a button on the dash, and the KLEF radio station played soothing classical music. "This should help you sleep."

"Hope you don't mind me using your coat for a blanket." She kept hers on but needed something to cover her legs. She reached in the back to retrieve his yellow and black down winter parka.

She snuggled under the jacket, inhaling his familiar pine scent. It comforted her and made her relax, while the hum of the car's engine lulled her to dreamland.

"We're here," said Nick, switching off the engine.

Macy's lids fluttered open to see the Denali Peaks Lodge just outside of Talkeetna as the sunrise splayed orange and neon pink over the mountains. "I love this place. Is this where everyone is staying?" She stretched and yawned.

"Some crews are staying here to film landscape for filler, but the rest of us are going up the road apiece to Foraker's Roadhouse and Kennel to film the sled dog scenes."

"Oh, I used to go there with my parents. Long time ago." She hesitated. "Will I be staying here or—will I be going to the sled dog kennel?"

"You're coming with us to Foraker's Roadhouse. DeMello wants you in more scenes as a good friend of Victoria's character." He leaned toward her. "I worked with the script supervisor to write your role into the sled dog scenes."

"Really?" Macy placed a hand on her heart. "You did that for me?"

EVERYBODY LOVES POLAR BEARS

"Your character's name is Stephanie Stevens, and you'll have lines in the next couple of scenes. You'll also get film credit."

Macy's eyes rounded. "Seriously? I'm no longer Woman Number Six? What made DeMello decide to give me a speaking part?"

"Victoria likes your spunk, and so does DeMello. She's taken a shine to you ever since you prevented her from becoming an iceberg in Polar Pond. And DeMello thinks you're good on camera." Nick sent her a look that ate up whatever leftover hostility she may have had toward him.

"Wow! I got a promotion from the background to a featured extra, and now I have a speaking part." She couldn't believe Nick had done this for her. "I don't know what to say. It's something I've always dreamed of." She reached across the console and squeezed his arm. "Thanks for doing that, Nick."

"I figured you'd like that," he said, opening his driver's side door. "You've earned it."

"Hey, Westwood."

He twisted to look at her. "Yeah?"

"You're making it difficult not to like you." She opened the passenger door. "Oh, and another thing... I hope you don't expect me to sleep with you as a return favor. Because I'm all about earning my way in this business."

"You've made that clear before. I expect nothing." He pointed his keys at her. "See, I was right. I knew you hated me."

"No, not hate. I detested you. Then scaled back to disliking you," she clarified.

"And now? You still dislike me?" His azure eyes sparkled.

"How can I go on disliking you for saving my life?" She laughed and got out of the car. She was glad she shared the ride today with him. It had turned out to be one of her better choices, and this warmed her.

Macy couldn't wait to see what the rest of this movie had in store, now that she had a bigger role and was getting along with Nick. She hoped at the very least that they would remain friends. She was unwilling to hope beyond that since they were still worlds apart despite their shared Alaskan background.

Nick had bared his soul, taking a significant risk in doing so. She knew that entrusting her with his vulnerability was a profound demonstration of faith.

That meant everything, and she wouldn't let him down.

Chapter 19

Nick helped the crew prepare for the day's film shoot at the Talkeetna lodge. He directed them to capture stock footage of the beautiful Alaska Range, then arranged for a leased helicopter to take them up for the perfect aerial shot. No drone could do the job—Nick wanted to showcase the best of Alaska on the screen, and only humans could make that happen. He was sure the result would be spectacular as he framed it in his mind.

As he worked, Nick let his mind wander back over the previous week. DeMello had given him more directing responsibility, something he appreciated. To his surprise, things had gone smoothly with Victoria and Dylan's love scenes. Since the movie was a family feel-good story, Nick directed Victoria and Dylan to keep love scenes sweet and clean. He'd filmed multiple takes when Victoria couldn't control her giggling when Dylan slid into steamy territory.

Overall, things were going well. He wouldn't obsess about Macy's discovery about his real background and identity. Macy was right; he'd already established credibility in the fickle film business. Frankly, he was tired of his charade. If people found out, let them.

After Nick finished his instructions with the Unit C crew at the Talkeetna lodge, he and Macy bundled up and headed to the parking lot for their drive up to Foraker Roadhouse. As they strolled together, he sensed a profound tranquility and a lightness in his step, as if the weight of the world had lifted.

"Zippo arranged for Baby Snowflake to be transported from Anchorage to film this scene with Dylan, Victoria, and you," he explained. "It's easier to film it here, though the movie setting is on the coast of the Arctic Ocean."

Macy gave him a doubtful look. "There are too many trees here. Hate to break it to you, but there are no trees along the coast of the Arctic Ocean."

"I know that, and you know that, but most audiences won't," he said with a dismissive gesture. "We'll get rid of the trees when we edit."

"Why go to the trouble to shoot on location if you can change the setting with special effects?" she asked. "If that's the case, we could have filmed these scenes in Anchorage."

Nick's boots bit into the snow, squeaking it. "It's better to come up here. There's more snow, and this is where the sled dog teams run."

"But why include a sled dog scene?" Her twin peak lips begged to be kissed.

He didn't dare, after what she'd said about earning her own way and his unwavering statement that he expected nothing. Crushing on this woman might be tougher than he thought. He chose the safer route of sticking to business.

"DeMello wanted one because his opinion is that audiences can't get enough of dogs in movies. So, he wrote this scene in, where Dylan's character rushes the injured polar bear cub to a vet after a wolf attack."

The sun glimmered her hair with streaks of copper as it cascaded from her furry ear muffs. "Did you get the sides I emailed you for the upcoming scene?"

"Yep." She held up her phone. "And I memorized my lines."

He moved close to look at her phone. "I'm impressed."

"I don't have that many, so it wasn't a big deal." She bumped him with her shoulder. "Besides, I'm a professional. So, Bruce Wayne, tell me what to expect in this next scene."

He tossed her a side-eye. "The gist is, even though you're a reporter, you've befriended Victoria's character," explained Nick. "You'll help Victoria and Dylan rescue the orphaned polar bear who gets injured by a pack of wolves. You and Victoria will help Dylan load the cub into the sled so he can mush him to the veterinarian with his sled dog team."

"Will the cub be sedated? He seems to scare easily," said Macy as her gloved hand bumped his.

He instinctively reached for her hand, then remembered himself and shoved it in his pocket. "Don't worry, Baby Snowflake's front paws will be wrapped for his fake on-screen injuries. His handler assured me he's been working with him to stay calm."

"Hope so." When she smiled at him with those luscious eyes, he wanted to scoop her up and do unmentionable things.

"Do you realize your speaking role will qualify you for an actor's union membership?" He liked that he'd helped make this happen for her, and in his view, she'd more than earned it.

"Really?" She hesitated and looked straight ahead. "Not sure I'll be able to afford the annual membership fee, though."

"You will once you get more work in other movies." He could help her, but only if she wanted it.

"That would be amazing." Macy stopped next to the passenger door of Nick's SUV.

"Hop in. It's six miles to the musher's cabin," said Nick.

They climbed into his rental, and each admired the unobstructed view of Denali Mountain.

Nick glanced at her. "Denali always leaves me awestruck."

"As it should. Our family used to win lottery tickets to drive into Wonder Lake each September after they closed the park to tourists. Some of my fondest memories are of those trips." She stared wistfully out the windshield.

"My mom and dad took us kids on those lottery drives, too. Now it's hard for Alaskans to get tickets because of the lower forty-eight competition."

Nick noted the mid-morning sun peeking over the Talkeetna Mountains just as he spotted the turnoff to Foraker's Roadhouse and Kennels. The sun's rays angled through the windshield, lighting up Macy's face as she scrutinized her phone. He figured she was studying the scenes for today's shoot, so he stopped talking to let her concentrate.

The cast and crew snaked their trucks and vans painstakingly along the curvy, snow-packed road. Finally, they reached their destination. The sled dog musher's kennel and roadhouse sat in the middle of a snowy meadow. Enclosed kennels, colorful dog houses, and a sizeable dog lot sat on one side of an expansive log home. A beautifully carved sign stretched across the top: *Foraker's Roadhouse*.

A cacophony of barking greeted the cast and crew as they piled out of their vehicles. The sled dogs wagged tails and yipped as a stout man with a curly white beard appeared on the covered porch.

"Welcome to Foraker's Roadhouse," he said with a jovial grin. "DeMello, my man, it's been a long time." His arm shot out in a familiar greeting, much to Nick's surprise.

"Sure has, Tommy. Haven't been back since we filmed *Denali Dogs* with your sled dog team. What year was that, anyway?"

EVERYBODY LOVES POLAR BEARS

DeMello strode up the long cedar steps to shake his hand and give him the requisite man-slap on the back.

The portly man adjusted his UAA Seawolves baseball cap. "Fifteen, twenty years ago, maybe?" he replied with a smile that crinkled his crow's feet.

This was news to Nick. DeMello hadn't mentioned he knew this musher. The two men shook hands, and DeMello motioned to the cast and crew milling around the front of the lodge.

"I'll make introductions. Here's our L.A. crew. Everyone, this is the famous Tommy King, Iditarod winner several times over." DeMello motioned at the two movie stars. "And of course, you recognize Victoria Miracle and Dylan Ford."

"Ah yes, I've seen you in a movie or two," said Tommy, his eyes turning to slits as he smiled. "Come meet the wife. She'll show you to your cabins. I run a lodge business for tourists who want sled dog adventures." He winked at Macy and squinted. "You seem familiar."

"I was here with my parents about eight years ago," replied Macy. "My mother interviewed you for a story in *Alaska Magazine*. Betty Applegate?" She gave Tommy a hopeful look.

"Oh yes, I remember. Gracious lady and an excellent journalist. She always did an outstanding job interviewing myself and other winners of the Iditarod Sled Dog Race. How is Betty?"

"She passed away four years ago. Pancreatic cancer," said Macy matter-of-factly.

"Sorry to hear that," said Tommy. "She was a lovely lady. Didn't your dad work for the Alyeska Pipeline Company?"

"Yes, but he's also gone. Right after Mom died."

Tommy gave her a grim nod. "So sorry. Your folks were good people. Real Alaskans."

"Yes, they were," said Macy proudly, catching Nick's empathetic expression.

Tommy glanced at DeMello. "Ready to do some filming while we still have daylight? If so, I'll hook up the sled doggies."

"That would be great," said DeMello, looking at Nick. "What do you think?"

"Yep. Let's do it." Nick turned to Macy and lowered his voice. "I'm so sorry about your mom and dad. I didn't know."

She shrugged. "Thanks, but it's been a while."

"Doesn't make it any easier. I also lost my mom to cancer." He gave her an empathetic smile.

"That sucks," said Macy. "Sorry to hear that."

While the technical crew got to work, Mrs. King beckoned Victoria and Macy. "Come with me, and I'll show you to your cabins. They're in back of the lodge."

Macy gave Nick a little wave as she and Victoria followed Mrs. King.

His eyes drifted to her spectacular ass in the same skinny jeans he'd tugged off her the day she'd fallen into the pond.

"Beautiful view, isn't it?" Zippo had sidled up to him.

Nick tore his gaze away from Macy's backside and regarded his Unit C director. "Takes your breath away."

"I presume you're talking about Denali Mountain, right?" Zippo gave him a lopsided grin.

"What else would I be referring to?" Nick said defensively.

"Oh, nothing. Nothing at all," said Zippo, staring off toward the women.

"Come on," Nick said gruffly, stealing an ogle at Macy's disappearing derriere. "We have work to do."

Chapter 20

Mrs. King escorted Macy and Victoria along a wooden boardwalk leading to eight cabins nestled on the edge of the spruce and birch boreal forest. She swung the door open to the largest cabin on the left.

"This one is yours. Your director said you two would be sharing."

"I love this! It's so cute and quaint," squealed Victoria as she gaped at the rustic Alaskan décor.

A rocker made of snowshoes graced one corner, and an antler chandelier presided over a modest oak dining table next to a large picture window, with Mt. Denali and the Alaska Range as the backdrop.

"Glad you like it. Make yourselves at home." Mrs. King turned up the wall thermostat and moved to the door, pausing with her fingers on the doorknob. "If it gets too warm, lower the heat. If you need anything else, holler."

"Thank you," said Macy, smiling at Mrs. King as the woman stepped out and closed the door.

Macy sat on one of the queen beds. "Are you sure you don't mind sharing?"

Victoria sat on the other and bounced on it, as if testing the mattress. "I can handle a roomie for a night. It's gorgeous here. Will we see the northern lights?"

"If it's clear, we probably will. They were out last night." Macy rested her backpack on the chair and moved to the window just in time to see Nick strolling toward his cabin.

She craned her neck, pressing her nose against the glass to see which cabin was his. He entered one on the opposite end, and she watched the door close behind him.

Victoria came up behind her. "You like our little Nicky, don't you?"

Macy feigned innocence at her comment. "Oh, no...I was just taking in the whole majestic mountains thing."

"Right. I've seen how you look at him." Victoria's mischievous grin flamed Macy's cheeks. "After all, you were naked with him. I envy you for that," she purred.

"As if I remember any of it," Macy said dismissively. "I wanted to crawl into a grizzly den and die."

"For what it's worth, I appreciate you shoving me out of the way, even though you fell into the pond." She crossed her arms. "I think that was supposed to happen."

"What do you mean?"

"You know how they say everything happens for a reason? Let your hair down a little with Nick. It doesn't take rocket science to see that he likes you."

"He was such a dick in the beginning," groused Macy.

"That's his deal. He acts like that when he's shy with people. I know for a fact he was attracted to you the second you two met." Victoria rose to dot lip gloss on her full lips in a round wall mirror.

"No way," Macy snorted. "Is that what he said?"

"No, but I could tell. Nicky and I are good friends."

"How good?" Macy asked hesitantly.

EVERYBODY LOVES POLAR BEARS

"Don't worry, we haven't done the boom-boom. I tried but couldn't get him to surrender to my charms." Victoria lifted her lips to wipe the lipstick from her front teeth.

A knock on the door commanded Macy's attention, and she moved to open it.

Nick filled her view. "Everyone is meeting in front of the lodge. We're starting the scenes. Tell Victoria."

"I heard you, honey!" Victoria called out from behind her.

"Thanks, we'll be right out." Macy smiled and closed the door.

"Told you, my dear. Go on ahead, I'll be there momentarily." Victoria rose and headed to the bathroom. "Need to freshen up first."

Macy scanned herself in the mirror. She stepped outside, surprised to see Nick waiting for her.

What a vision he was with his rugged face, untamed golden hair, and turned-up coat collar against Alaska's most impressive backdrop of Mount Denali. His gray wool scarf draped around his neck as an afterthought, framing his chest like an outdoor magazine ad. Nick embodied the tough, manly Alaskan vibe Macy had known all her life; he had the confident, purposeful stride that was characteristic of guys up in this neck of the woods.

You can take the man out of Alaska, but you can't take Alaska out of the man.

"Ready for some movie fun?" Nick held up his rolled-up script.

Macy produced her own copy. "Told you before, I'm a consummate professional."

"That you are. I like that you're prepared." She hadn't seen Nick in this good of a mood the entire time she'd worked with him. His calm energy painted the air in bright hues; he must be in his element.

As they reached the side of the house with the wide dog yard, Macy took in the flurry of activity—crew members setting up lighting rigs, camera operators adjusting lenses, and dogs barking wildly in their kennels.

DeMello strode up to Nick. "The dog team is ready to go! We'll show Dylan how to mush first. Tommy will handle the team for the long shots; then we'll do the close-ups of Dylan on the dogsled and film him starting and stopping before we put Baby Snowflake inside the sled with him. We'll do a quick shot with the cub, then stick the stuffy in the sled for the distance shots."

Macy guffawed. "A what? He's kidding, right?"

Nick gave her a solemn look. "No. We always use big stuffed animal toys for distance shots." He darted a glance at the animal protection representative who stood off to the side, observing the action with her ever-present clipboard.

Macy tried to match Nick's seriousness, but after he stepped away to direct the action, she burst out laughing until tears rolled.

"What's so funny?" asked Victoria, appearing beside her.

"They're using a stuffy for the distance shots." Macy wiped tears from her cheeks with her gloved finger.

Victoria looked at Macy like she'd slid off a flying unicorn. "We always use a stuffy for those shots. Why use a live animal when a fake one will do?" She looked like a snow goddess instead of a marine scientist, decked out in white to match the snow.

Macy was aware of the ongoing conflicts between animal protection groups and Alaskan sled dog racers. It was always in the news. People from the lower forty-eight who were passionate about animal rights frequently accused mushers of cruelty to run sled dogs. Macy thought these criticisms revealed a significant misunderstanding of the sport because Huskies were born to run. It also amused her that most of these people had never visited Alaska.

Tommy winked at the woman, then climbed into the sled to show Dylan how to position himself and hold on. He reviewed the mushing commands—hike meaning run, whoa meaning stop—then motioned Dylan to climb on so he could practice maneuvering it.

"I'll yell the commands because the dogs know my voice," explained Tommy. "Then we'll have you do it. Sound like a plan?"

Dylan seemed nervous as he gingerly stepped up onto the sled and grabbed hold of it. Macy saw his reindeer-in-the-headlights expression, and Nick offered to help him.

"Okay, buddy, let's review." Nick patiently went over it again with Dylan. "Now tell me what you're going to do. Convince me you're an expert at this."

In Macy's estimation, Nick would make a good elementary school teacher, with his steady patience and thorough instruction. He talked to Dylan as if he were a child, only without condescension. Dylan didn't seem to mind. He was intent on Nick's every word.

Dylan's swagger amused Macy as he bellied up to the dogsled to become an Alaskan musher for the lens. She compared him to the man standing next to him. In her humble opinion, Dylan Ford didn't come close to Nick's chiseled features and the confident, efficient way Nick handled himself. Nick would be the star of this film if rugged masculinity were the ruling factor. She wondered if he had acting experience. She hadn't thought to ask.

"Holy crap, what's happening?" she muttered to herself. "Am I crushing on Nick Westwood?"

Don't do it. It can't lead to anything.

DeMello ordered the crew, "Get some shots of Dylan standing on the sled, then we'll get him on the move." He glanced around and got the ready-to-go nods from each of the crew. "Okay, roll 'em. Action!"

When they finished filming the closeups, DeMello wanted Dylan to mush the dogs down the trail leading from the dog yard. The trail led off between rows of tall spruce on either side.

"Take it slow," coached Tommy, standing next to Dylan. "Ready?"

Dylan nodded, though Macy suspected he wasn't at all ready. He seemed petrified.

When DeMello called 'action,' Dylan yelled, "Hike!"

The sled dogs lurched ahead, jerking the sled so hard, Dylan flew off. He swam through the air in slow motion before face-planting into the deep snow.

Everyone waited with bated breath, but there was no movement.

Chapter 21

Macy covered her mouth upon seeing America's hottest action star lying spread-eagled in the deep snow, like Da Vinci's Vitruvian man. She waited for Dylan to move, but he lay there motionless, like roadkill.

Nick hurried over to Dylan. "Hey, bro, are you alright?"

"Get a stunt double for this," Dylan grunted angrily, then pushed off from his face plant. Snow stuck to his hair, eyebrows, and eyelashes. He pulled an insulated glove off with his teeth and brushed snow off himself.

Dylan wasn't amused. "You can't expect someone who's never been on a dogsled to control these damn dogs!" he ranted. "This is ridiculous! I want a stunt double. Now!"

"Calm down, Dylan," DeMello said impatiently. "You'll get the hang of it."

Nick turned toward DeMello. "Mind if I handle this?" he said out the side of his mouth.

DeMello made a wide, sweeping gesture. "Be my guest. Apparently, you're the only one he listens to."

Victoria had walked up and stood next to DeMello, nodding her head. "That's true, Nicky. He does."

Nick flicked his eyes at Victoria, then strode over to Dylan. He took him aside and placed his hand on the temperamental actor's shoulder, speaking in a soothing manner.

Macy leaned against a four-wheeler, watching the action. She couldn't get over what a calming effect Nick had on Dylan. He'd calmed her, too, in recent days, though she'd been too stubborn to admit it. His was the faraway voice that had penetrated her haze that day at Polar Pond. She'd been so cocooned in her own judgmental bias where Nick was concerned that she hadn't seen this side of him.

Or maybe she had but choked on her own denial, refusing to believe it. She was ashamed of her narcissism, where Nick was concerned. Now that she was aware of this, she beat herself up at how she'd treated him in the past. She made a firm resolution to make things right with him.

She couldn't hear what Nick was saying, but something he said in his quiet tone softened Dylan's shoulders and made him relax. The movie hero's pained look dissolved as he glanced at the ready-to-run Alaskan Huskies, who stood wagging, waiting for humans to get their act together.

Nick man-slapped him on the back, then moved to the dog team. "Come here, Dylan, let's pet the dogs." Nick motioned to him and scratched one husky behind the ears.

The husky leaned into his touch, and the sides of his mouth turned up. Macy's turned up as well.

Who says dogs don't smile?

"Scratch their ears like this," instructed Nick. "Alaskan Huskies are smart animals. They know when you're nervous. Show them you're relaxed and that you are in charge. Okay?"

"Yeah, okay." Dylan hesitated, then scratched another husky, who stood happily wagging.

"Let's get everything positioned again for another take. We're burning daylight and must get this done, okay, bro?" Nick

EVERYBODY LOVES POLAR BEARS

continued talking in a calm voice to Dylan while Tommy backed up the team of eager dogs to the start position—no easy feat for eight eager-to-run Huskies.

Nick waved Dylan over. "Hey, buddy, I have an idea. Get back on the sled like I showed you," he ordered. "I'll get behind you to control the dogs. Once we get going, I'll step off so you can drive by yourself for the cameras. Okay?"

Dylan's eyes widened in panic. "No! Don't leave me alone on this contraption! Can't you duck down or something?"

Macy almost felt sorry for the beleaguered actor until she remembered the millions he makes from these films. She wouldn't be nearly as patient.

"Suck it up, Ford," she said under her breath. "Where's Tom Cruise when you need him?"

Nick wiggled his hand in a come-on gesture to the fearful action star. "Come on, climb aboard. The dogs know what to do. After we get the shot, I'll catch up to you and halt the team. You've got this."

Reluctantly, Dylan climbed onto the dogsled. Nick positioned himself behind him, then reached around Dylan to grab hold of the sled with both hands. He twisted to address the cast and crew behind them.

"Victoria and Macy, take your marks and wave as we take off. Dylan, your job is to relax and act like you're in charge. Zippo, get ready with the cameras. Let's film this. Marker!" shouted Nick.

A crew dashed out with the digital clapper board and snapped it shut.

"Hike! Hike!" Nick called out, gripping the sled around Dylan.

The sled dogs responded with an excited yip as they sprinted down the trail. Nick drove the sled a short distance before jumping off so the cameras could record Dylan piloting the dog team by himself.

"Get this rear shot!" Nick hollered at Zippo, who worked the rear camera.

Zippo trained the camera on the sled as it disappeared down the trail.

Macy and Victoria stood on their marks, waving after Dylan with enthusiasm.

"Cut!" hollered Nick, enthusiastically. "Print it! Mind if I use your four-wheeler?" He asked Tommy, who stood watching his dog team.

"Go ahead!" Tommy called back, motioning to the vehicle a short distance away.

Nick hopped on the four-wheeler and took off to halt the dogs.

"Brilliant!" erupted DeMello with a radiant face. "Westwood does it again. We'll edit the polar bear cub into the shot. Didn't think Ford would have a tough time doing this." He clapped his hands in approval, smiling at everyone.

"Woo-hoo, go Nicky!" hollered Victoria.

Nick's expertise impressed Macy on how he'd handled the situation.

When he caught up to the dog team, he hollered, "Whoa, Huskies!"

The dogs slowed to a stop. Nick hopped out of the vehicle and moved to the lead dog. He grabbed hold of the gangline that connected the dog team, then moved to Dylan and slapped his shoulder. He gestured to the four-wheeler, and it looked like he wanted Dylan to drive it back.

Macy could tell by Dylan's body language he hadn't a clue how to drive a four-wheeler.

EVERYBODY LOVES POLAR BEARS

"Macy!" hollered Nick. "Can you give us a hand?"

To her surprise, he asked for her help over anyone else's. Then again, he probably thought she was the only one who knew how to drive a four-wheeler. She jogged up to Nick and Dylan.

"Can you drive the four-wheeler back to the start position?" asked Nick. "I'll mush the dogs."

"I'd really appreciate it," intoned Dylan, smiling at her.

"Sure thing." She moved up to Nick, who was turning the dog team around, leading the lead dog by the harness. "You've done this before, too, haven't you, Westwood?"

A corner of his mouth lifted. "Can't get one past you, can I? Thanks for helping with this, Applegate. Meet you back at the start. Don't forget Dylan." He gestured at the ragged-looking actor, who looked as though he'd wrestled a dog team instead of driving one.

"Climb on," said Macy, motioning for Dylan to climb aboard the four-wheeler. She cranked the engine and swung the vehicle around, driving it back as Nick asked. She parked and hopped off, moving to DeMello.

"Are you happy with the takes Nick got on film?" Macy wanted to make sure Nick got the credit for all that effort.

"More than happy." DeMello greeted her as she climbed off.

"If you want a sled dog team wrangled, it takes an Alaskan to do it." As soon as it slipped from her mouth, Macy realized she probably shouldn't have said it in front of everyone—especially DeMello.

"Westwood handles sled dogs like a seasoned musher," said DeMello, watching Nick skillfully mush the team back to them.

"If anyone could get Dylan to mush those darn dogs, it would be Nick," said Victoria. "One would think he'd done it before.

Pretty good for a born and bred Angeleno, eh?" She stared straight at DeMello, who nodded.

Macy gave her a startled look.

Victoria shot a knowing glance at Macy, which told her Victoria either knew or she'd just figured it out. Either way, it was nice of her to cover for Nick.

"I mean, how would anyone from L.A. know how to mush dogs, anyway?" Macy back-pedaled, wanting to crawl into a snowbank after spilling the beans.

Nick Westwood was the glue that held this entire production together, and she'd blown his dirty little secret.

Chapter 22

Nick breathed a sigh of relief after they'd wrapped for the day. He'd returned to his cabin, cherishing the quiet after his busy day. He enjoyed having a cabin to himself. His stomach growled, and he looked forward to seeing what Tommy and his wife had prepared for dinner.

He stepped into the cozy, warm lodge, inhaling the aroma of roasted meat, sauteed vegetables, and baked bread that sent his stomach grumbling for a taste. Two long tables stretched out in the spacious dining area of the main lodge. The crew had gathered at one and the actors and directors at another.

Nick scanned the room and spotted an empty seat next to Macy, but Dylan claimed it before he could. Nick reluctantly sat across from her, seething about the way Dylan shamelessly flirted. The food appeared, steam rising from oven-roasted vegetables with a carved moose roast in the center.

DeMello rose from his seat at the head of the table, holding a glass of wine.

"I'd like to toast you all," he declared with booming enthusiasm. "I'm especially impressed with the Alaskans on this cast and crew. You've been nothing but professional, making our jobs easier. Thank you." He raised his glass of wine, and everyone lifted their glasses.

Macy chimed in. "Thank you for bringing your film project here and giving us these wonderful opportunities." She caught

Nick's sapphire gaze, disarming her with his irresistibly devastating smile.

"We'll be making more films in Alaska," responded DeMello, clinking glasses all around the table.

"The scenery here is exceptional," Dylan piped up, eyeing Macy as he lifted his wineglass. "Westwood, I'm impressed with how you handle a dog team. Where'd you learn to do that?"

Nick couldn't get past Dylan ogling Macy. He knew damn well what was on Dylan's mind. A guy could always tell when another wanted into a woman's pants.

Nick had prepared for this inquiry. "I mushed with my cousins years ago." It was true, only he'd done it down on the Kenai Peninsula with his own team of sled dogs, not up here, in Alaska's Interior. He caught Victoria and Macy's knowing glances.

Each time Nick tried talking to Macy, Dylan cut him off with some lame story about himself. Nick still didn't know what had happened the night Macy had dinner with Dylan. He'd wanted to ask her about it on the drive up here but decided against it since they were just beginning to get along.

He knew one thing about Dylan—if beautiful women didn't show interest, it only fueled his desire. Bedding them down was a conquest for Dylan Ford.

Nick only hoped he'd never become that pathetic.

When dinner ended, and after everyone helped to clean up, Tommy produced a guitar and headed to a piano across from the crackling fire in the enormous fireplace.

"Who is up for making music?"

Zippo rose from his chair and ambled over. Tommy offered him the guitar, and a woman took the piano bench and fingered the keys.

EVERYBODY LOVES POLAR BEARS

Tommy produced a fiddle and lifted it. "Does anyone play?"

The script supervisor ambled over and accepted the offered fiddle with the bow.

"You all start, and I'll follow," said Tommy, tuning another acoustic guitar. "I played in a band a long time ago, believe it or not. Used to play at the Alaska State Fair in Palmer, headlining for big bands, like the Doobie Brothers and Kansas." He grinned at the group. "You youngsters are too young to know who they are."

Zippo cocked a brow and fingered the intro to the Doobie Brothers tune, "Black Water." The fiddler joined in with the string intro, and the woman on the piano turned around to sing.

"Oh my gosh, I love this song," said Macy. "A band played this song on a Mississippi River steamboat cruise I took when I visited New Orleans last year."

Nick loved how she was like a little kid in a candy store. He admired her childlike innocence, unlike other women he'd known who'd lost theirs somewhere along the way.

When the song finished, the musicians launched into more tunes, some recent, some classic rock. Everyone was on their feet dancing. Even DeMello got up and danced, taking turns with Victoria and Mrs. King.

Dylan stood and grabbed Macy's hand. "Dance with me," he commanded.

Nick watched Dylan execute his smooth moves on Macy, laughing and talking as if he was really into her. Nick couldn't tell if she was falling for it or not.

When the musicians took a break, more wine flowed, and DeMello reminded everyone they had to get up early to film—his hint not to imbibe too much. Nick drank little these days. After losing Gloria years ago, he'd climbed into a bottle, then dragged himself out when he left Alaska to pursue a film career.

The music started again, and Zippo plucked the beginning of an Eric Clapton tune and crooned, "Wonderful Tonight."

Before Dylan could steal Macy again, Nick swooped in. "Want to share this dance?"

She smiled at him. "Thought you'd never ask."

Nick pulled her to her feet and noticed how her eyes glinted gold. When Macy placed her hand on his shoulder, he saw that as a positive sign. He clasped her other hand and slid his free hand down to her waist. She tensed, then gradually relaxed and followed his lead. When she green-lighted his move, he pulled her tight against him.

He spoke into her ear. "Thanks for helping me today. I figured you'd know how to drive a four-wheeler." The firelight cast her skin with a golden, ethereal radiance that even a lighting designer couldn't achieve.

She laughed. "Heck, I've been driving three and four-wheelers since I was five."

"Ha, me too. We used to ride them next to the Kenai River back when we fished for kings." He chuckled with the happy memory.

"Wished I would have known you when you lived up here. How long has it been since you've caught a king salmon?" she asked, with a twinkle in her eye. "Or aren't you into combat fishing?"

"Too long," he murmured. "I'd love to come back this summer and fish on The Peninsula. I'm an expert wrangling crowds on riverbanks while combat fishing—same as I am at wrangling hundreds of movie extras."

EVERYBODY LOVES POLAR BEARS

"I'll bet you are. You should come up this summer," she said promptly. "Maybe you can shoot another movie up here, and then you could stay—" She stopped short, and he waited for her to finish. Instead, she blushed.

"I would love that." The thought of coming back up excited him beyond measure. It gave his new plans a mental boost.

"I have a confession," she said haltingly. "Today, when you helped Dylan and Tommy with the sled dog team, I told DeMello it took an Alaskan to handle one." She furrowed her brow. "I think I mistakenly outed you. I'm sorry."

Nick chortled. "I don't care anymore. It was a dumb idea to continue that charade. Anyway, it no longer matters."

The music stopped. They stilled, with their arms around each other. Nick didn't want to take his hands off her, especially when he saw Dylan watching. Macy slid her palms from his shoulders, and he reluctantly let go.

DeMello spoke up. "Well, folks, time to get some shuteye so we can hop to it first thing in the morning. It'll be another long day. Thank you, Tommy and Mrs. King, for the fantastic meal and wonderful music." Everyone said their thanks and donned winter gear for the quick jaunts through the deep snow to their cabins.

Nick put on his coat and helped Macy with hers. "I'll escort you to your cabin," he offered as she put on her hat and mittens.

Dylan breezed up, looking like a Yeti bundled in his faux fur jacket and hat. "Miss Macy, how about an after-dinner drink in my cabin? What do you say?"

"Sorry," Nick cut in, his hand on the small of her back. "We have some things to go over for her scene tomorrow with Victoria."

Dylan narrowed his eyes. "What is there to go over? All she has to do is stand around and look sexy." He winked at her.

"Well." Macy stiffened and drilled him with a glare. "That was slightly inappropriate. Ever hear of Me Too?"

Nick jumped in. "Better apologize, good buddy. You don't want another sexual harassment complaint. Your union frowns on such things." His eyes locked with Dylan's in a stare-down.

Dylan dropped his gaze to Macy. "My apologies for that remark. Still, if you stop by my cabin later, I can explain in more detail." He gave her a sweet smile and hurried out the door.

"That guy is a piece of work," she murmured with a lifted brow. "Goes to show you. Looks aren't everything, right?"

"Not in Dylan's case." Nick shook his head. "I don't mean to tell you what to do, but I will anyway...don't go to his cabin. He only wants one thing, and only the prettiest women qualify."

"I figured. Geez, some things never change." Macy gave him a playful look. "Then again, I was thinking of sleeping my way to the top."

"I wouldn't advise that, Applegate," he teased back. "It leads to nowhere." And he meant it.

They strolled along the shoveled, frosty boardwalk leading from the lodge to the cabins under the starlit sky. The snow illuminated their way, along with the soft glow of a bright moon. Jagged mountains loomed like commanding shadows in the distance, their imposing silhouettes a reminder of this magnificent wild land.

Nick pointed. "Check out the snow on the Talkeetnas. The peaks are like snow cones all lined up, ready for strawberry syrup."

"I prefer blueberry." She stopped, her frosty breath puffing out like a bubble blower. "You couldn't ask for a more enchanting backdrop for this movie."

EVERYBODY LOVES POLAR BEARS

A brisk breeze tousled Nick's hair, and he instinctively lowered his chin to shield his nose and mouth from the biting cold. "It's nippier up here, away from the coast." The chill seeped into his bones.

She clutched his arm and pointed. "Look! Right above Denali!" Her voice carried a mix of wonder and delight.

Following her focus, Nick took in the spectacular sight. An ethereal display of the Aurora Borealis danced across the night sky, a neon green with hints of purple and a delicate shade of blue swirling gracefully over the majestic Alaska Range. The northern lights framed Mount Denali in a celestial halo, illuminating her with an otherworldly glow on this clear, crisp night.

"Magical, isn't it?" Nick fixed on the riveting spectacle as memories flooded back. "When I watched the northern lights as a kid, I believed they brought me good luck." Nostalgia took hold, reliving his childhood moments.

"I always thought the Aurora had magical powers," Macy said softly, her face turned toward the heavens.

"I always made a wish." A hint of vulnerability crept into Nick's voice as he closed his eyes. But he didn't mind; he trusted her.

"What do you wish for?" she asked softly.

He opened his eyes to see her gazing up at him, the lights dazzling her lovely pools of green. His warm breath mingled with the frosty air.

"If I tell you, it won't come true, now, will it?" He thought about kissing her. Instead, he took her hand and gently squeezed it. "Come on," he said, leading her along the snowy path.

A mix of emotions welled inside of him. Uncertainty loomed on the horizon because he was unsure what the future had in store, so he savored the present. The rest would have to take a back seat for now.

This amazing Alaskan woman had more in common with him than he'd realized. Maybe someday he'd tell her what he wished for.

But not now—not when he had big decisions to make.

Chapter 23

Macy turned to Nick as they stood outside of her cabin, tilting her head at the unmistakable sounds of lovemaking emanating from inside.

She put a finger to her lips. "Listen."

Uninhibited moaning punctuated with an occasional 'yes, yes!' reached their ears, causing Macy and Nick to grin at each other. She brought her hand up to stifle her giggles.

"Sounds like Dylan caught up with Victoria," Nick said drily. "He scored after all."

"I can't go in there," said Macy with a shrug. "I don't want to interrupt them. Guess I'll stay out here and watch the Aurora until they're done."

"That could be a while. Come to my cabin to wait it out." He held up his gloved hand. "Don't worry, I'm not Dylan. I won't hit on you."

"We've moved beyond that, don't you think?" Her heart fluttered like hummingbird wings.

They hadn't been alone together except for the drive up here. After admiring Nick's sublime patience and giving nature earlier today, Macy wanted time alone with him. She wanted to know more about him and his life growing up in Alaska.

"I was thinking the same, but glad you said it first." He smiled at her. "Come on, follow me. Better than standing out here freezing."

She followed him to the last cabin, nestled among the snow-laden spruce.

Nick swung open the door, reached in to flip on an overhead light, and stepped back for her to enter. "Come in, make yourself at home."

Macy walked inside. One wall displayed a massive king salmon, while another showcased a caribou and a bull moose with impressive antlers.

"This is definitely a sportsman's dream. Our cabin has bright colors and lacy décor, while you have all the dead animals." She tugged her knit scarf from around her neck.

"I don't mind. I used to hunt moose and caribou." Nick closed the door. He removed his coat, stocking cap, and gloves and hung them on a wall hook. He removed his boots and set them next to the door.

He glanced at Macy, then moved to the wood stove and squatted next to it. "While I light a fire, get rid of your winter gear and make yourself comfortable."

She tugged off her coat and boots and arranged them next to his. There was something intimate about doing that, and it tugged her heart a little. She stood in the center of the spacious cabin, glancing around at the colorful, realistic Fred Machetanz paintings that showcased lazy polar bears lying on ice floes. Her gaze rested on the humongous bed with its own zip code, big enough for a musher and his dog team.

"The polar bear paintings are good karma, don't you think?" She motioned at two of them, one with a mother bear and her cub, another with a bear zonked out, snoozing on blue ice.

Nick straightened after he got the fire going. "I love Machetanz's art. My dad gave me one of his paintings of sled dogs.

EVERYBODY LOVES POLAR BEARS

Did I mention I had a sled dog team back in high school? Always wanted to run the Iditarod."

She nodded. "I figured you had mushing experience when I saw how you handled Tommy's dog team today."

Nick ran his fingers through his hair. "Never got around to distance racing, but it brought back some fine memories." He stared at the paintings for a long moment.

She cleared her throat, and he snapped back from wherever he'd gone in his head. "Do you have anything to drink?"

"I have sparkling water. Hopefully, not frozen." He opened the back door of the cabin and retrieved a beverage can from the back porch. "Alaskan refrigerators. Here you go."

"Thanks." She gratefully accepted it and stood on the braided rug in front of the woodstove.

Nick flipped off the overhead light. "A good fire is all you need to properly light a cabin."

He finger-combed his tousled hair on his way back to where she stood. His primping radiated a masculinity she found sexy. Towering in the firelight, he appeared rugged and wild, like he'd just finished taming grizzlies and cavorting with wolves.

"Didn't know I was so thirsty." Macy sipped the slushy water, scrutinizing Nick as he bent to stoke the fire. Watching him do this mundane task, after what he'd done with the sled dogs and his patience with Dylan Ford—she viewed Nick Westwood in a new light.

Once the fire took off to his satisfaction, Nick closed the screen door of the wood stove, leaving the cast iron door open so they could watch the flames. The firelight cast a cozy amber glow throughout the room. He rose and stood next to her, forearms bare under his rolled-up sleeves. His red and black tattoos gave him an exotic vibe, while the firelight flickered across the five o'clock shadow on his jawline.

He dropped his gaze to her wool socks, where her big toe peeked through a hole. "Your toe must be cold. It's blue."

"That's my aqua-blue nail polish." She laughed and stooped to pull the sock over her protruding toe. "Or did you think it was frostbite from when you fished me from the pond?"

"Aren't we paying you enough to get socks without holes?" he teased.

"Hey, don't judge my sock collection. I bet you have plenty of holy socks. Oh, wait... Hollywood people don't have socks with holes," she jibed.

"Only if it's trendy. Hey, there's something I'd like to know." He shifted his weight to the other foot. "Why didn't you like me at first? Or maybe you still don't like me."

"I like you just fine." Macy stared at the licking flames. "But you were rude and arrogant at my audition."

"That's it? Thought I'd done something really offensive—like strip you down and lie naked with you or something." He took the can of sparkling water from her and sipped.

Macy snatched the water back. "Do you mind? I don't know where your mouth has been." She meant it as a joke, but it came out sounding suggestive. Her cheeks heated.

"It's just that I'd worked so hard to prepare for my reading. When you didn't let me finish, I figured you thought my reading sucked."

Nick blew out air. "That didn't mean you weren't good, just that I saw what I needed to. I'm good at fast assessments of skills and talent." Nick scratched his head. "Auditions were exhausting. I wasn't supposed to be auditioning people, but the loser they hired for a casting director turned out to be a sloth. By the time you showed up, my brain had numbed."

"Well, you came across as an arrogant jerk," she contended, though her opinion of him had risen after what she'd witnessed about him in recent days.

"I'm an Alaskan, for cripes' sake. How can I be arrogant?"

"Well, you were." She turned and caught his Hollywood-handsome profile in the amber glow, and her breath hitched.

"So, what were your other reasons for hating me?"

"I never said I hated you. I said I didn't like you. There's a difference."

He leaned sideways. "You didn't seem to dislike me when you kissed me in the church."

"I was acting!" she countered. "Besides, you kissed me first. I was being a team player so Zippo could set the lighting."

"Uh-huh, so your tongue in my mouth was in the spirit of teamwork." He crossed his arms. "Still think I'm a jerk, even after helping you at Polar Pond?"

"You weren't a jerk *that* day when you pressed your slightly nude body next to mine." Though it had been in a different context, her mind raced with this vivid image, causing a rush of heat through her veins.

A spark of firelight caught his eye. "Ha, you make it sound erotic. But if I hadn't warmed you like I did, you might have had a more serious outcome. I did the same for my little brother one spring when his kayak flipped on Tustumena Lake, down on the Kenai."

Macy's jaw dropped. "Oh, no. Was he okay?"

"He's still above ground." He paused. "I was afraid he'd die, and how would I tell our parents? All of that ran through my head when I pulled you from Polar Pond."

"You mean dip-netted me," she corrected. "I'm sorry you had that flashback."

He smiled. "You still haven't answered my question. Do you still think I'm a jerk?"

"Not for *that*." She gave him a direct look. "But yes, for firing Andrew."

"Oh, so that's it." Nick's head bobbed up and down. "I figured you were miffed about that."

"And why do you suppose that was? It's not that you fired him. I understand why you had to. But you humiliated him in front of everyone. That was a terrible thing to do." Macy squirmed as she recalled Andrew's crushing moment.

"I had to set an example. We can't have actors taking photos on set. You know that," he said sharply. "I didn't enjoy doing it. I'm not a sociopath. You make it sound like I'm Annie Wilkes from *Misery* or Norman Bates from *Psycho*."

"Those movie characters are bona fide psychopaths. You'd better not be one of those." She folded her arms. "I'm sorry, but I don't appreciate what you did to Andrew."

Nick nodded. "Okay, I get it. What do you want me to do? Hire him back?"

"What could it hurt? He's a talented actor, and he was so excited to get a part in the movie. I'm sure he's learned his lesson and won't violate his NDA again."

Nick hesitated. "If it means that much to you, I'll think about it. But rules are rules."

EVERYBODY LOVES POLAR BEARS

"I understand, but I'd really appreciate it," she said. "On a brighter note, you impressed me today with how you worked with Dylan."

"None of us expected he would freak out at mushing sled dogs. I mean, he's an action star." Nick bent to stoke the fire with a cast iron poker, then returned it to its stand.

"Speaking of Dylan, I've been wanting to ask you something," he ventured. "That night you had dinner with him at the Captain Cook—did you—did he—you know, put the moves on you?"

"Why on earth would you ask me that? Because he invited me to his cabin?" His words walloped her like a slap. "So, you want to know if I slept with him?"

"I know it's none of my business—"

"Darn right, it's none of your business!" she cut in, her voice louder than she intended. "Why do you want to know?"

"Well, did you?" he persisted with an accusing stare.

"Not until you tell me why you want to know." She steadied her gaze. "Is this a deal breaker for you?"

"Maybe."

"I don't believe this! Why should I tell you, of all people, about my sex life? You know what? I'm going back to my cabin." She strode over and grabbed her coat and boots.

Before Nick could open his mouth, she'd vanished out the door.

Chapter 24

"Macy!" Nick called after her. "Wait a minute!"

She resisted turning around. She didn't appreciate being questioned about her sex life by anyone—least of all by the assistant director of *Everybody Loves Polar Bears*.

Then again, Victoria and Dylan were probably still going at it in her cabin.

Nick jogged up and planted himself in front of her. "I didn't mean to offend you. I—I just wanted..." For once, the suave and debonair Nick Westwood was at a loss for words.

She fixed him with an unwavering look. "What business is it of yours what I do on my own time? You're my boss on the movie set, not in my private life. I can't believe you asked me that when I hardly know you—"

Nick abruptly grasped her shoulders and devoured the rest of her words with a kiss. When he finished, he drew back. "Sorry, but that's the only way I can get you to listen."

"Isn't that a bit dramatic? All you had to do was tell me to listen." Her dazed expression made him laugh.

"I tried that." He grinned.

She glanced down at his stocking feet. "Get inside before you get hypothermia and I have to strip *you* naked."

"I wouldn't say no to that," he said jokingly, taking her hand and hurrying her back to his cabin.

EVERYBODY LOVES POLAR BEARS

She stepped inside to the cozy warmth. She knew why he'd asked her about Dylan. She wasn't clueless, but she wanted to hear him say it.

"Okay, for the record. I didn't have sex with Dylan Ford," she said, her eyes fixed on the flickering flames. "When a group of women came over to our table and swooned all over him, he didn't even notice me get up and leave."

Nick moved up to stand beside her. "Hope that didn't mess with your ego."

Macy guffawed. "Icons we admire from a distance rarely turn out to be who we thought they were. Who you see on a screen isn't what you get in real life. Makes me think I admire the wrong people." Nick's proximity clouded her thoughts when his pine scent reached her nostrils.

She moved to the window to distance herself and caught the last remnants of the Aurora Borealis streaking across the black, starry skies.

Nick stayed where he was. "I apologize for being intrusive. You must know by now that I'm attracted to you."

His words wrapped her heart in a warm embrace, but the best way forward was honesty.

"Something you should know." Macy turned around and leaned back on the windowsill. "I don't use sex to get what I want. I've worked hard to develop my acting skills. I either have what it takes, or I don't." She paused. "Besides, empty-headed pretty boys hold no interest for me."

Nick gazed out the window with her. "Do you think I'm empty-headed?" He slanted a disarming smile that raced her pulse and messed up her brain.

What is it about him that does this to me?

"No, but you are kind of pretty." Truth be told, she'd been afraid to let herself become attracted. It had been easier to convince herself she didn't have feelings for him.

"I'm also good at reading people," he murmured, his voice dropping.

"What are you reading *now?*" She turned toward him. "Do I look like someone who dislikes you?"

"You look like someone who needs to be kissed." Anticipation spun her senses as he closed the space between them. She was helpless to throttle back the dizzying current speeding through her.

When their lips met, her heart virtually broke free of her chest. She loved every hormonal pulse his kiss sent through her. She wrapped her arms around his neck, feeling his warmth and the stubble on his chin.

Now that she had Nick Westwood in her arms, she couldn't get enough. She'd wanted this ever since their first kiss, but it'd taken an eternity for her heart to convince her brain this was something she wanted.

No denying him now. She was too far gone.

His arms encircled her, pulling her tight against him, and their lips continued the delightful rhythm of giving and taking, the way she loved kissing. He was darn good at it, too. Her heart jettisoned around the Big Dipper as she let herself melt into him.

Nick broke the kiss. "Been wanting to do that since the day we kissed in that church."

"Me too," she whispered, fastening her gaze to his fiery one.

"Why didn't you say something?" His arctic pools peered into hers, jangling her insides.

She swallowed. "Why didn't *you?*"

EVERYBODY LOVES POLAR BEARS

He tugged her into him so tight, his heartbeat vibrated her insides. She gasped as his lips slid down the side of her neck, unleashing a flood of suppressed feelings.

There was no going back after this. No flipping way.

"Oh, Nick..." Macy moaned, gasping when he touched her breast over her sweater. She wanted his hand *under* her sweater. Just as her fingers closed over his, there was a loud, urgent pounding on the door.

They jumped like kangas off a scorching wood stove.

"Holy cripes, the timing sucks," Nick spoke against her lips, then let out a disgruntled sigh. He held up his finger. "Hold that thought." He moved to the door and opened it a crack.

"Where's Macy?" demanded Victoria, pushing the door open.

"What makes you think she's here?" Nick failed miserably at lying and was an absolute flunky at playing innocent.

"Oh, for pity's sake, I wasn't born yesterday." Victoria poked her head around the door, then pushed it wider to step inside. "There you are, Bear Woman. Time to come home."

"Hi, Victoria." Macy straightened and smoothed her hair, noticing Victoria eyeballing their stocking feet.

"I see you got comfortable." Victoria rolled her eyes. "Oh, stop it, you two. I know what you were doing. Sorry about that tiny delay." She jerked her head toward her cabin as if referring to a late flight arrival. "I should have gotten a cabin to myself. I'm a woman with needs." She wrinkled her nose at Nick.

Macy didn't know whether to feel amused or irritated.

"Nick was nice enough to let me hang out here until you were—um, finished." She retrieved her coat and boots and put them on.

"How thoughtful of you to lend a hand to one of your subordinates," said Victoria in a suggestive voice.

"I couldn't let her stand out there and freeze to death," Nick said simply, shrugging.

"I'm here to save you from the clutches of this sex maniac," she sniffed at Macy. It was obvious she and Nick knew each other well.

Macy hoped not *too* well.

"Thanks, Mom," Macy teased. "Don't know what I would have done."

"Me neither," said Victoria, lifting her chin. "Come along now, Bear Woman. You need your beauty rest."

"Goodnight, sweet Nicky." Victoria tapped his cheek and stepped outside, her breath in little puffs of frost. "You know DeMello's rules. Do your hanky-panky when we finish filming in this godforsaken wilderness."

"Right back atcha, sweetheart," retorted Nick, his mouth twitching.

Victoria put a forefinger to her lip like she was genuinely thinking. "Hmm, guess I'm a rule breaker, aren't I?" She gave Nick a demure smile.

"Goodnight." Macy interjected, raising her mittened hand to him in a toodle-oo. It seemed like a trite gesture after their intense make-out session.

Nick held the door with a glacier-melting smile. "See you in the morning. Oh, and...act casual. You know the drill. This never happened."

"Why does everything have to be a big secret? All right, I know the drill." Macy desperately wanted to kiss him again, but she dutifully scooted out the door after Victoria. She floated from one virtual cloud to another, her soul swirling around Denali's summit.

EVERYBODY LOVES POLAR BEARS

"It seems we both scored tonight," purred Victoria, with her cat-eyes aimed at Macy as they ambled to their cabin.

"Oh, no—I didn't score. I mean I didn't—he didn't—we didn't—" Macy sounded like a penitent Girl Scout as she eyed the elegant, voluptuous movie star she now considered a friend.

Victoria chortled. "Relax. No need to explain. I know more than you think I do." Victoria rested her gloved hand on Macy's shoulder. "Please don't break Nicky's teensy little heart. He is so dear. I knew early on he was from Alaska, though I never let on. I thought it was cute the way he hid it."

"That was nice how you didn't out him to DeMello today. Unlike I did," said Macy, opening the door to their cabin. Thankfully, Dylan was gone.

"Of course, I wouldn't out him. I love our little Nicky." Victoria followed her in and closed the door. "I tried to snag him into bed, but he wouldn't have it. I've seen the way he looks at you, and I'm jealous." Her mouth twitched.

"I won't break his heart if he doesn't break mine," Macy surprised herself with her admission.

Did she have herself a movie boyfriend? Like the way actors fell for each other while filming a movie: Brad and Angelina, Winona and Johnny, Blake and Ryan? Except Nick wasn't an actor, and she wasn't a movie star.

But she loved the romance aspect just the same.

Her resolve not to let Nick Westwood break her heart hung in the air like the free-spirited Aurora in the endless Alaskan skies.

Chapter 25

Nick noted that filming the rest of the sled dog scenes took longer than expected, with darkness insisting on cutting into the afternoon. Snow had fallen, adding a dramatic touch to the shoot, one that DeMello wanted to take advantage of.

Nick was uneasy about how thick and fast the snow was coming down. When the wind kicked up, he knew they'd better get back to Anchorage or risk being snowbound in Talkeetna. He didn't want the production to fall behind on their tight film schedule.

"We'd better get the trucks and vans out of here," Nick said urgently to DeMello, who whistled for everyone to speed things up.

Nick and Macy helped load personal items and film equipment into the trucks and vans for the snowy drive back to Anchorage. Nick wasn't too worried; all the vehicles had studded snow tires that bit in for better traction.

He told DeMello and the rest to go on ahead while he stayed behind to settle with Tommy for the lodging and the use of his sled dog team. Macy had volunteered to stay with him, and he was glad for her company, especially after last night when they'd talked out their differences. He was relieved that she now liked him. Maybe a little more than that if he was lucky enough.

Though it had been an unwelcome interruption last night, Nick was relieved it had been Victoria and not DeMello banging on his door—knowing his boss frowned on cast and crew getting involved.

"Make love like rabbits all you want once filming is over, but no shenanigans until then," he'd repeatedly told the production crew. "We can't afford the distraction."

Nick went inside the main lodge with Tommy while Macy started his SUV. He watched her out the window, clearing snow from the vehicle and meticulously cleaning the wiper blades. It struck him like an Alaska Railroad train engine—he'd fallen for this feisty actress and he didn't see any way around it.

Mrs. King appeared from the kitchen, holding her cellphone. "Received a Nixle from the Alaska State Troopers. The Parks Highway is closed because of a pile-up. Even if you make it to Talkeetna, you won't reach Anchorage anytime tonight."

Nick heaved a sigh. "I meant to check the forecast, but with the hectic film schedule, it slipped my mind."

"You and Macy should hunker down here tonight. I'll get you out in the morning after I've plowed the road," said Tommy.

"Are you sure we won't be a bother? We don't want to trouble you." His eyes drifted to Macy, waiting patiently in the passenger seat of his idling SUV.

"No trouble at all. It's better than the two of you getting stuck or stranded on the Parks Highway overnight."

"I'll talk to Macy." Nick put on his coat and stepped outside into the blowing snow, which was once again sticking to the side of his vehicle. He swung open the passenger door. "Guess what?"

Macy held up her phone. "I know. The Parks Highway is closed. We aren't going anywhere, are we?"

Nick shook his head. "Tommy thinks we should stay put tonight." He knew this would cause a delay in filming, so he did his best not to sound happy about it.

"When is our call time on set tomorrow?"

Nick shrugged. "Whenever we get there. The rest of the cast and crew are no doubt stuck on the highway unless they stayed in Talkeetna. Let's grab our gear and head back inside, and I'll text Zippo."

They pulled their packs and duffels from the SUV and hauled them up the snowy steps back into the lodge. Once inside, they removed their coats and boots, shaking off the snow.

Tommy had finished feeding his dogs and followed Macy and Nick into the house. "Weather forecast calls for blowing snow. In Alaska, that means a blizzard." He stamped his feet and removed his boots before heading into the living room.

"It's already blowing sideways," noted Macy as Nick's phone pinged a notification.

"It's a text from Zippo." Nick tapped it.

We're all hunkered at the Talkeetna lodge. Are you coming?

Nick thumb-tapped a response.

Macy and I are staying here. See you tomorrow when the roads open.

Zippo responded with a thumbs-up emoji. Nick held his phone out to Macy. "They're all staying in Talkeetna."

"Wise decision," said Macy, nodding.

The unexpected break secretly delighted Nick. He glanced at his watch, then peered out the window. "It's five p.m. and dark as ravens in a cave. Time flies when you're having snow."

EVERYBODY LOVES POLAR BEARS

"Have a seat at the table. The Missus usually has dinner ready by now." Tommy motioned for Macy and Nick to sit at the beautifully sculpted spruce table.

"Thanks for feeding us and letting us stay another night. Next time you're in Anchorage, I'll return the favor." Macy smiled.

"I may just take you up on that, young lady." Tommy's eyes crinkled with his infectious grin. "It's no bother. We're glad for the company."

Everyone bantered about the fickle wait-a-minute weather in Alaska's Interior. Nick had missed these quirks about his home state. It pleased him not having to go anywhere for the rest of the evening.

"Is DeMello working you people hard?" Tommy eyed them both as he rolled a toothpick to the other side of his mouth.

Nick chuckled. "No more than usual. Filming in Alaska's winter has its challenges, but I'm glad he's asked me to help direct this movie."

"I watched you today. You should direct your own movies." Tommy breathed on each lens of his glasses, then rubbed them vigorously.

Mrs. King sailed out of the kitchen, wiping her hands on her apron. "Let's get some warm food in you. I have moose stew and merlot." She breezed to the kitchen and returned to the dining room with two steaming bowls.

"Mmm, that smells good," said Macy, inhaling the tantalizing aroma.

Tommy rose to help his wife. He placed a bowl of hot rolls on the table, along with a bottle of merlot. "We'll get you two out in the morning once I plow the road. Taking the dogs to the vet in

Talkeetna. I can take one of you in the sled, and the other can drive your rig with the Missus."

Macy lit up. "How fun! What do you say, Westwood?"

"Actually, if you have a pair of cross-country skis I could use, I'd love to skijor behind a dog or two," volunteered Nick. "Have any of your dogs pulled cross-country skiers?"

"Daisy and Aphrodite can do it. They're wheel dogs, but steady runners. They pull my sons when they come home to visit. Not my leader dog, though. He'll yank you down and drag your ass through the snow." He bent to peek at Nick's feet. "I'm sure my son's cross-country shoes will fit you."

Nick locked gazes with Macy. Each time he looked at her, it was as if he was falling off a cliff in a freefall—and he couldn't care less whether he hit bottom.

"I didn't know you skied cross-country," gushed Macy. "But of course, you did, growing up on the Kenai."

Her enthusiasm warmed him in places he couldn't afford to be warmed in right now.

"You're an Alaskan?" Tommy boomed out, passing the rolls. "DeMello said you were originally from L.A."

"I grew up in Soldotna, actually." It felt good to say it out in the open. Nick flicked his eyes to Macy's, who nodded her approval.

He stood to pour wine into everyone's glasses, then sat back down and lifted his wineglass. "Here's to being snowed in. And I'm not the least bit sorry. In fact, I'm elated." And he truly was—for all kinds of reasons—especially for the reason sitting across from him.

"I'm with you on that one, Westwood." Macy lifted her wineglass, and he clinked it.

EVERYBODY LOVES POLAR BEARS

No matter how old Nick would grow to be, or how many years would pass, this was the exact moment he'd forever mark in time: the moment he fell head over heels in love with Macy Applegate.

He envisioned a digital clapperboard snapping this scene marker. Only no one would yell, "Cut!"

At least he hoped not. He wanted this scene to extend into the next season... with ongoing sequels.

Never to be canceled.

Chapter 26

Macy enjoyed sitting with Tommy and Mrs. King by the crackling fire in the lodge. While this brought back memories of doing the same with her parents in their Anchorage hillside home, all she could think about was being alone with Nick. Her insides fluttered at the thought there would be no one from the cast or crew to interrupt them tonight.

Her thoughts became wicked, and they turned her on.

Nick glanced in her direction. "I think I'll head to my cabin. Need some shut-eye for tomorrow."

"Me, too," Macy said quickly, pretending to yawn. She rose and stretched, feigning exhaustion. She followed Nick to put on her winter gear, masking her excited anticipation with a neutral expression.

Mrs. King escorted them to the door. "I changed the sheets in both your cabins." She smiled sweetly, glancing from one to the other. "Sleep in if you like. It'll take my husband a bit of time to plow the road."

"Thank you so much, Mrs. King. We appreciate your generous hospitality. Goodnight." Macy stepped off the porch into knee-deep snow on the boardwalk, gripping the wooden handrail to steady herself in the blizzard. Gusts of wind blew stinging flakes at her cheeks as Nick came up behind her.

"You're such a suck-up," he said teasingly.

She whirled at him. "Oh, and you aren't?"

EVERYBODY LOVES POLAR BEARS

"I'll go ahead of you and break trail," he volunteered, moving to the front of her, his bunny boots pushing through the snow like miniature snowplows.

"Thanks, Westwood. You're a true gentleman." She squinted through the hurricane flakes stinging her face as Nick trudged ahead of her.

When the log cabin emerged from the whiteout, Macy tugged off her mittens and tucked them into the pocket of her parka. She scooped up a handful of snow and formed a round, hard ball, then launched it with lightning speed at Nick's back.

He stilled and tipped his head back. Quick as a snowshoe hare, he bent and gathered snow for a retaliatory attack. His fast pitch torpedoed her chest.

She staggered backward, pretending to gasp for air. "Can't breathe!"

Nick straightened like a prairie dog on alert. "Are you okay? Sorry, didn't mean to hurt your... lovelies."

When he closed in on her, Macy had a snowball on the ready and nailed him. Hard. "Ha! Fooled you, Hollywood! Don't worry, my girls didn't pop. They aren't fake L.A. boobs. They're real Alaskan ones!" She hurled another snowball that would have nailed his man parts if not for his down jacket protecting them.

"Saved by the coat!" He laughed, pitching a snowball, hard and fast.

She leaped sideways, dodging a direct hit. A gust of wind pelted them with snow, and they bolted toward her cabin.

Nick got there first and stood with his back to the door. His chest heaved from exertion. "Here's the deal. You can stay here, or..." He made a wide, sweeping gesture. "You can come to my cabin, enjoy the pleasure of my company, and lay on soft furs with a warm, cozy wood stove."

Macy toyed with him, curious to know how badly he wanted her to go to his cabin. "I appreciate your offer, but I'll stay in my own cabin. I've been wanting some time to myself." She reached around him for the door handle.

He caught her wrist. "Liar. You'd rather stay here alone? Where a crazed bear might smash down your door or a pack of ravenous wolves could gnaw their way in?"

"I can protect myself." Her thoughts spun in circles as she gazed up at him.

His eyelash caught a snowflake and held it hostage. She found that endearing.

"Not like I can." The way he said it made her tingle, and she had the urge to launch herself at him.

Instead, she gave him a direct look. "Convince me, Bruce Wayne."

"I'll do more than that." He grabbed her parka and tugged her close for a long, sensual kiss.

Snowflakes tickled her nose as he swirled his tongue around hers. He finished his kiss with soft nips on her lower lip, then picked her up and carried her off to his cabin like a mail-order bride.

"Open the door. My hands are slightly full." He nodded at the handle.

She reached down and opened it, and Nick carried her inside and set her on her feet in the middle of his cabin. He closed the door, and when he slid the bolt to lock it, the sound of clicking metal upticked her pulse.

EVERYBODY LOVES POLAR BEARS

They were finally alone. For real, this time. She couldn't believe he'd swept her off her feet and carried her to his cabin, like in the movie *Seven Brides for Seven Brothers*.

She stood where Nick put her as he removed his coat, boots, and baseball cap, and shook the snow from his hair. He moved to the window, combing his hair with his fingers, watching the snow swirl outside.

He turned around with hands in his pockets. "Are you convinced?"

"If I wasn't, I wouldn't be standing here." She'd never felt more certain about anything.

Nick was quite a sight, standing rugged and masculine in the snow's soft reflection from outside the windows. His partially shadowed face only enhanced his alluring Alaskan vibe.

"Take off your coat."

"Don't you ever get tired of directing?"

"Not something like this." His voice dropped as he took a step toward her.

"Sorry, Batman. I'm directing this scene." She pulled off her stocking cap and tossed it on a chair, keeping her gaze fastened to his. They stood for the longest time, watching each other.

Realization hit Macy like a thunderous crack of ice calving into the ocean, sending shock waves rippling through her; she knew without a doubt she wanted Nick Westwood.

More than anything.

He moved toward the wood stove and bent to start a fire. She tried corralling her lust by taking deep breaths as she studied his perfectly shaped Hollywood tush.

"We won't need a fire," she said breathlessly, tossing off her coat and tugging off her boots. "We'll make our own."

Now *that* got Nick's undivided attention. "You're right. What was I thinking?" The underlying sensuality of his words overturned her heart.

She stepped to the zip-code of a bed, and lowered herself to remove her thick wool socks as sensually as she could, although there was nothing sexy about gray wool socks.

Nick moved close, and every cell in her body snapped to attention.

His eyes traveled over her. "I want to make love to you. But only if you don't expect a bigger role afterward." The corners of his mouth lifted, causing her to laugh.

She dropped her socks on the floor, then spread her arms wide in a comical gesture. "Hey, isn't that the point of doing this?" she teased.

"Not on my part." He pulled her to her feet and kissed her, his lips nipping at hers and teasing them with his tongue. His fiery kiss intensified, dipping her into erotic territory.

Macy moaned and hated breaking the kiss, but she wanted to take charge just like she said. She lifted her sweater over her head and tossed it. She then lifted Nick's sweater and his t-shirt underneath. Since she was too short to carry out her mission, Nick took over and discarded them.

"Oh, my God…" she trailed off, staring at his sculpted bare chest. She moved her palms over his soft skin, her fingers cresting every ridge and bump on his chest and abdomen. "I was at a slight disadvantage the first time we were naked," she murmured, inhaling his pure, woodsy scent.

"Now you have every possible advantage. I know you're directing this scene, but I have a suggestion. Maybe you could undress for me? I've already done it once." He gave her a mischievous look. "Just saying."

The intensity in his eyes made her crave him even more, and she slid her arms around his neck and kissed him. She knew what was coming. Her sense of urgency insisted she rush, but she needed to slow things down. This could be their only night together for all she knew.

Macy was determined to make it a good one.

Chapter 27

What an unbelievably passionate moment this was—the remoteness, the blowing snow, and Nick's salacious heat. This newfound intimacy with him was surreal. Macy's mind spun—she couldn't wrap her head around the fact she was about to make love with someone she'd formerly despised. How wrong she'd been to be deceived by first impressions.

Nick's unexpected display of affection had her all gooey inside. She hadn't undressed herself for a man this way and she trembled a little. With her gaze fastened to his, she unzipped her jeans and shoved them down, kicking them away. Momentary panic hit: *did I put on granny panties again this morning?* She blanked and couldn't remember. Judging from Nick's expression, she must not have—unless he had a granny panty fetish.

She glanced down to find she hadn't. Relieved, she turned her back to him. "Undo me. After all, you've done it before."

His fingers tingled every nerve ending on her skin as he unclasped her bra. He turned her around to face him, slipped his fingers under the lacy straps, and eased them slowly down, brushing his fingertips down her arms, leaving a trail of fire.

Goosebumps rose on her flesh, and her breath snagged on the sudden rush of air she sucked in. Macy turned to face him, and his cerulean eyes locked onto hers. She hesitated.

EVERYBODY LOVES POLAR BEARS

"Keep going, Applegate. You're directing this, remember?" His eyes drifted downward as she stood before him in her non-granny panties.

She slid her fingers to her waistband, then stopped. No need to rush...they had all the time in the world. Nick's heat was driving her insane, and she wanted to slow this to savor every sweet second.

"I appreciated you leaving these on the first time you took off my clothes." She smiled at him. "Now you have my permission to remove them and warm me with your body heat... again."

"At least your life isn't in danger this time." Nick dragged his fingertips along the top of her panties, then slowly lowered them to her ankles.

Macy heard his fast intake of breath and nearly came undone. "That's a matter of opinion," she squeaked out. Her life may not be in danger, but her heart sure was.

He pressed his lips tenderly to her neck and slid them to her earlobe, nibbling it.

She trembled, but not from the chilly air. His touch charged her with a longing she'd never known—not like this. The tender way he touched her sent heat coursing through her. Bumps rose on her skin like molten lava.

He lifted his head. "Let's get under the covers, and I'll warm you. Just like old times."

"I'm all for that." She reached down to unsnap and unzip his jeans.

"Except this time, you're naked and awake." He flung back the sheet and the goose-down comforter, then eased her onto the bed.

She grinned at him. "Better than naked and afraid."

Nick's steady gaze bore into her with silent expectation, his jeans hanging open, slung low on his hips. One gloriously sexy vision. She mentally photographed him to create a virtual poster to tack onto the wall of her brain.

He disposed of his jeans and crawled in beside her, lifting the thick, cozy comforter over them...and trailed kisses down her throat, driving her insane. His hardness pressed into her thigh, and she reached down to touch him.

"I want you, Viktor Andreanoff."

"Who is that guy, anyway?" he teased, stroking her hair. "I've wanted you ever since you walked in to audition. Sorry, I acted like a dickwad, but I had to hide what I was really thinking." A package ripped, and he sheathed himself.

"And what was that?"

"How I wanted to make love to you. Like this." He guided himself to her entrance and covered her mouth with his own. He took her gently, and she welcomed him, heart, body, and soul.

Macy threaded their fingers together as he increased his tempo. She let out a moan, then a louder one, and filled the cabin with the sound of her pleasure. All the roller coaster feelings she'd had for him surfaced—how she'd despised him until he'd gradually won her heart—one piece at a time. Now, in this moment, Nick Westwood had captured the last piece—and she gladly let him have it.

"Oh, Nick!" she cried repeatedly, with a mind-bending peak of release.

As her private northern lights' explosion catapulted her into euphoria, Nick moved faster until he stiffened and shuddered as he followed her to release.

Together they stilled, his heart beating against hers. She couldn't remember the last time, if ever, that she'd had such an intense, intimate experience with someone.

EVERYBODY LOVES POLAR BEARS

When Nick moved to lift himself off her, she clutched him. "Stay inside," she breathed.

Macy wanted him to know what was rolling around inside of her heart while he was inside of her. She wanted to pour out her devotion to him, share her innermost secrets, then shout his name from the summit of Denali.

Instead, she rubbed his back as they both spiraled down. "I love your warmth, but you're rather heavy."

He kissed her, then rolled off her onto his back and took her hand in his.

She swiveled her head toward him. "Should we have done this? We work together. Maybe we shouldn't have—"

"Yes, we should have," he said firmly. "Why are you second-guessing?" He pulled her tight against his side. "Don't worry, you aren't sleeping your way to the top, if that's what you're worried about. Not with me. That's not how I roll."

"But this will look bad. I mean—I'm a nobody actress having sex with the movie director."

"No, Macy Applegate is making love with Nick Westwood—a regular Alaskan guy," he corrected, turning her chin toward him. "And you aren't a nobody. Not to me."

"But everyone will think—"

He cut in. "No one will think anything unless you tell them. No one needs to know. Besides, screw what anyone thinks."

"But Victoria knows that we—you know—kind of like each other."

"Like each other?" He laughed. "What is this, lunch in the West High School cafeteria?"

Nick propped his head up on an elbow. "Forget the movie bullshit for a moment. This feels right to me. Decide what is right for *you*."

Macy tried to sort her confusion. "That's the thing. This *does* feel right. But I have mixed feelings about us."

"Why? Because you started out disliking me?"

"Yes—no, I mean, I don't know." How could she put this, so he'd understand? "I need to be sure I'm making love with you for the right reasons—and not that I'm crushing on you because of your celebrity and that you're technically my boss as the director of this movie."

"Assistant director," he corrected. "And I'm no celebrity. Wait a minute—you're crushing on me only because of my movie position?" Disappointment laced his tone.

"No, that's not what I meant! Please, don't misunderstand," she rushed to explain. "It's just that... I want to be sure, that's all."

"Sure about what?"

"I don't have random sex," she said nervously. "And you're so hot and everything. I only do this with people that...that..." Her words tumbled out until they glommed into a hot mess in her throat.

"Look, Macy, don't overthink this. You're safe with me." He pulled her tight against his side. "Everyone thinks intimacy is about sleeping together. It isn't. True intimacy is when you can share your past and your truth and admit your screw-ups without someone judging you or wanting to change you."

He stunned her with his revelation. "Oh, my God. You're not at all who I thought you were... not in the least." She turned her head to gaze into his eyes.

EVERYBODY LOVES POLAR BEARS

"I'm glad you finally accepted the real me. I just needed the chance to show you."

Macy hesitated, wanting badly to tell him her soul-baring truth—that he was someone she could trust—someone she could love. But only if her love was for all the right reasons, and not a sophomoric crush because of who he was and how he made a living. Uncertainty held her back.

She had to be certain.

"I'm glad you showed me the real you," she said finally, choosing her words carefully. "All right, I won't overthink this."

A few weeks ago, Nick Westwood was the last person on the planet she wanted in her life. But now... why couldn't she tell him he'd become the happiest intrusion into her life? What else was holding her back?

Maybe because she feared tonight would fade into a distant dream once she and Nick were back in the everyday life of reality. So much was at stake: his career, her hopes of changing hers, and the success of the polar bear movie.

Uncertainty gnawed at her like a wolf on a bone.

Only time would tell.

Chapter 28

Early the next morning, Nick breathed a sigh of relief that Tommy had plowed the road as promised. He'd set Nick up with two sled dogs to pull him on cross-country skis. It had been a long time since Nick had skijored behind dogs and he was excited to get started.

"Hike! Hike!" Tommy's voice echoed through the crisp winter air as he commanded his sled dog team of ten to move forward, their paws kicking up snow. Macy hunkered inside the dogsled as the team pulled them toward Talkeetna. Nick had arranged a heavy Hudson Bay blanket around her to make sure she was all warm and cozy.

He followed the dogsled on his skis, delighted that the musher and his dog team broke the trail for him. Mrs. King brought up the rear in Nick's SUV rental, leaving him plenty of room to ski.

Nick reflected as the sled dogs pulled him along, something he hadn't had the luxury of doing since he couldn't remember when with his whirlwind film schedule.

Last night had been spectacular, and Nick was glad he'd talked Macy into staying with him. When they'd cleared the air, he realized how he'd negatively affected her when they first worked together. He'd even appreciated Macy calling him out on his pretending to be a born and bred Angeleno.

Nick liked his surprising new intimacy with her. At first, it'd bothered him when she'd said she wasn't sure if she only liked

EVERYBODY LOVES POLAR BEARS

him because of his movie position. But then he hadn't minded too much when he remembered her hotness comment. He'd taken that as a compliment. At least she liked him, which was better than before.

She'd turned his life upside down in just a few short weeks, and in doing so, she'd changed his perspective; he saw things clearly for the first time in a long while. He'd been deliberating for months, years—what it was he wanted to do with his life—and he'd finally arrived at a decision.

It was time to follow his dream of independent filmmaking rather than work for others on these big film projects, where he was just another cog in the Hollywood machine. He'd gained enough knowledge and experience over these past several years to make it happen. He couldn't wait to share his decision with Macy.

Before wrapping *Everybody Loves Polar Bears*, he'd talk to DeMello about becoming an independent filmmaker. Nick knew DeMello wouldn't want to lose him as his right-hand man, but Nick also knew DeMello would want him to succeed, and not talk him out of it.

Filming would end soon, and everyone involved with this production would scatter to the wind. After forming bonds with cast and crew, a film wrap was always a sad time for him.

Of course, there were those that he never cared to see again. A certain swaggering box office heartthrob came to mind—no love lost there—but mostly it was hard to say goodbye to everyone. Even Victoria. He wasn't sure he was prepared to do that yet.

A sudden idea hit him. Maybe after they wrapped, he could take Macy to the family home, the twenty-acre homestead his dad had left in Nick's care down on the Kenai Peninsula. The spectacular setting would be the perfect backdrop for them to spend time together and get to know each other.

Tommy eased the sled to a gentle stop in the snow-covered parking lot of the Talkeetna Lodge. Nick followed on cross-country skis behind two dogs, swishing through the powder in a peaceful rhythm. He loved being back on skis, same as when he lived in Alaska.

Mrs. King rolled Nick's SUV to a stop in the parking lot of the lodge where they'd filmed two days ago.

"Whoa!" Nick commanded the two dogs, who immediately halted, happy panting tongues hanging out the sides of their mouths. He removed the nylon tow line from around his waist.

"How'd my skis work for you?" Tommy stepped to Nick, wiping his brow. "These are two of my best Huskies." He scratched one under the chin, and the dog wagged his tail.

"The skis worked great, and so did the dogs," said Nick, planting his ski poles into the snow. A symphony of snow angels chorused in his brain as Macy clambered from the dogsled and approached.

"You're a natural!" she gushed.

Nick loved the enthusiasm in her voice. He beckoned her over with a mischievous grin. "Come here, Applegate."

She moved to him, and he laid a kiss on her as if they were alone in this vast wintry landscape. His heart tripped over itself like a drunken sailor until Macy pulled back and shot a nervous glance at Tommy and Mrs. King.

EVERYBODY LOVES POLAR BEARS

Tommy laughed. "Don't worry, we didn't see anything." He tended to his dogs and helped his wife settle inside the sled to continue their mushing trip into town.

Nick stepped out of the cross-country skis, then helped Tommy lash them to his dogsled. He turned to Macy. "I'm not worried. Even if DeMello were standing here, I'd still kiss you."

Macy gaped at him in open-mouthed surprise. "I highly doubt it. You'd worry what your L.A. peeps would think. You even disowned Alaska for them, remember?"

"Things have changed...I've changed." He removed his sunglasses to wipe them off. "Besides, we'll finish filming in a few days. Then it won't matter." He didn't know what was next for him and Macy, but he refused to think about it right now.

"I was wondering if we could talk about that," she said haltingly.

"We will. One thing at a time, okay?" A light breeze blew strands of hair across her face, and he brushed it back with his gloved hand. He stroked the ruff bordering her hood. "Nice parka. I admired it at your audition. Incidentally, I knew this was real fox fur."

"Can't put one past you, can I?" she said, gazing up at him.

"I know my Alaskan animals."

"Well, you're working on the right movie, then." She laughed.

Nick tugged off his stocking cap and combed his hair with his fingers. Frost stuck to his eyelashes, eyebrows, and the stubble on his jaw. He didn't wipe it off; this was a badge of honor for the completion of his rigorous skijor trip.

"Did you like your sled dog ride?" he asked.

"Yes! And I loved watching you ski behind us." Her smile lit his world because things were different today. *He* was different.

"It was exhilarating. Great to be on skis again in Alaska." Nick loved the pink staining Macy's cheeks in the crisp air under the bright morning sun. He had the urge to scoop her up and abscond with her somewhere to make love to her again.

After saying goodbye to Tommy and Mrs. King, Nick and Macy tucked themselves inside Nick's toasty SUV. He leaned across the console and cupped her cheek.

"Let's get something straight before we jump back into the fray. No matter what happens from now on, I've decided I want you in my life."

"Oh, you've single-handedly made that decision? Well, what about what I've decided?" she challenged.

"Which is?"

"I want you in my life too," she said simply.

That's all he needed to hear. He'd finally found the woman of his dreams. How to hang on to her was the new challenge, but he'd figure it out.

Better yet, he hoped they'd figure it out together.

Chapter 29

In the last few days of filming, Macy had fun playing it cool with Nick on the set. She loved it when their eyes locked, but only for a second, so no one would suspect anything. On one occasion, she pretended she had something in her eye when DeMello caught her winking at Nick. No one so far knew they were involved, except Julie and Victoria. Macy wanted to keep it that way until filming ended.

DeMello had found an extras supervisor, so Nick no longer wrangled the extras, and he seemed less stressed. Each night after wrapping, they'd have dinner together, and he'd spend the night in her bed. Macy loved getting to know him on a whole different level. He was witty and fun, not at all like his persona on the movie set, all stern and businesslike.

She figured him to be a Gemini with that dual-personality thing going on. When she'd asked him, he told her he was a June baby. There was no longer a cause for concern whether they'd continue seeing each other. As they neared the end of filming, DeMello announced the entire production would wrap by Valentine's Day.

Between the busy film schedule and their lusty evening activities, Macy and Nick had avoided discussing what would happen after the production wrapped. Both knew their worlds were miles apart. Not just distance, but their social and work worlds. While Macy had set her sights on a film career down south, now she wasn't so sure that was at all what she wanted.

She'd landed in a fairy tale with an uncertain ending.

Victoria had moved Macy into her dressing room. "Bear Woman has a calming effect on me, and she'll ensure that I wear the proper winter gear in this frozen wasteland of a wilderness," she'd sniffed to DeMello.

"Ready to freeze our hineys off in this outdoor night scene?" Victoria's proud brown eyes sparkled through thick black lashes as her hip-length white goose-down coat hung open with a miniskirt beneath it. Her stylish faux-fur hat that slanted to one side of her ever-bouncy blond curls, exposed everything but the side of her head.

Macy grimaced at Victoria's white patent leather thigh-high boots with stiletto heels. "You're not wearing those in ten-below-zero cold, are you?"

"How could you say that?" Victoria placed her hands on her hips with a death stare. "These are my Botega Vennetas. I got them in Milan."

"You'll freeze your hiney off. Designer boots are fashionable and look hot, but in Alaska your toes and girl parts will get frostbite. Did Julie advise you on what to wear?"

"I came up with my own choice for this next scene," Victoria said proudly. She eyed Macy's sensible *Xtratufs,* along with her long, down-filled sensible coat.

"You'll have to keep your feet moving so your toes don't freeze. The wind chill has dropped to fifteen below zero."

EVERYBODY LOVES POLAR BEARS

Julie poked her head in, holding up a pair of insulated snow boots. "Take these with you. I think you'll need them. Stay inside the van between takes if you insist on wearing those." She motioned at Victoria's questionable boot choice.

Zippo popped up behind Julie's shoulder. "Time to roll, sports fans. We must make this quick and get out of the weather."

"We're coming," said Macy, snatching a fleece throw from Wardrobe before hurrying after Zippo.

He led them towards the idling van outside, the exhaust swirling with exaggerated puffs in the extreme cold. The clear, crisp night had settled over the stillness of the cityscape. Soft streaks of light illuminated the ice crystals that hung in the frigid air, creating a ghostly atmosphere.

"Night scenes are the worst. And this one gives me the chills. Pun intended," said Victoria, peering out the passenger window. "It's bad enough filming in this dark, horrific cold, only to stroll along, meet a moose, and deliver a monologue about saving wildlife. Whose idea was this, Zippo?" She shot him a sidelong glance as she peered into a compact mirror, dotted on lip gloss, and snapped the mirror shut.

Zippo shrugged. "I do what DeMello tells me to do. I pushed back because of the subzero temps, but he wanted this scene filmed tonight."

"I bet I could have talked him out of it," pouted Victoria. "I hope it's an animatronic moose, at least," she fretted, tightening her cashmere scarf around her neck.

Macy used her phone to read her script. "No such luck. This one is the real deal, a bull moose from the wildlife conservation center. This says all we do is move along the sidewalk to the alleyway, and when we see the moose, you launch into your monologue about conserving wildlife." She shot Victoria a glance. "You know your lines, right?"

"Of course. I'm a professional," snapped Victoria. "All I can say is Bullwinkle better cooperate." She squinted upwards, wrinkling her face. "What's wrong with the streetlights? Are they upside down? The lights are shooting straight up!"

Macy laughed. "Oh, that's ice fog. It happens when ice crystals hang in the air. Looks cool, don't you think?" She peered up at the ethereal streams of light streaking up from the light sources, fading into the inky night.

Victoria looked her dead in the eye. "You people are crazy to live up here."

Macy chuckled. "We hear that a lot."

Zippo slowed the van, tires squeaking loudly on the subzero snow as the vehicle came to a halt in front of the Anchorage Log Cabin Visitor's Center. He'd arranged for it to be open so the cast and crew had a place to warm up between takes, except for Victoria and Dylan, who would warm up inside the idling van.

"Oh goody, we're here," groaned Victoria in a monotone.

Macy crossed her fingers that this would be a quick scene, but getting an unpredictable, uncivilized moose to cooperate with them might be a tad iffy.

"Oh God, why did I agree to do this?" groaned Victoria. She snatched the script from Macy and scowled at it, then dropped it on the console. "Let's get this over with," she muttered.

"Why isn't Nick directing this scene?" Macy asked Zippo as the women climbed out of the van onto a slick sidewalk, the snow squeaking beneath their boots.

Zippo shook his head. "DeMello has him filming filler scenes with a supporting cast on the Unit A shoot."

EVERYBODY LOVES POLAR BEARS

"Ha, clever how Westwood wiggled his way out of working outside in this gorgeous weather." Macy's breath frosted around her face.

"You two don't lop each other's heads off like you used to." Zippo zipped up his coat and put on heavy gloves. "You guys call a truce?"

"We still lop occasionally. Just not as often." Even thoughts of Nick weren't enough to warm her in this biting wind chill.

Zippo whistled at the cast and crew, his breath fogging in the frigid air. "All right, everyone, places. The handler has the moose ready to go. He's a trained moose, so don't worry. Let's do this as painless as possible."

"A trained moose?" Macy cocked a brow. Moose were anything but tame. In her experience, they were as wild as everything else that wandered through Anchorage and the surrounding wildlands.

"Where's Dylan? He's in this scene, too," said Victoria, her breath frosting in little puffs. She stomped her fashionable Italian designer boots, and Macy hoped her clueless friend wouldn't frostbite her toes.

"Right here," said Dylan's muffled voice as he emerged from his limo. Julie had bundled Dylan up so tight Macy could barely see his face beneath his scarf. "I won't last long in this cold. Let's get this over with," he grumbled.

Zippo strode up, wearing his headset. "The three of you will leisurely stroll on the sidewalk, then pause for a beat at the entrance to the alleyway when you see the moose." His breath clouded around him like smoke. "He'll be a safe distance away, and next to his handler, who'll be off camera. Victoria will deliver her lines, then Dylan and Macy react. Easy peasy. End of scene and we all go home."

"I can do this as long as Mr. Moose behaves himself," sniffed Victoria. "Br-r-r, let's get this show on the road."

Macy shivered. "February is always like this with the wind coming off Cook Inlet." She squinted up at the tall tower lights the lighting techs had positioned at the entrance to the alleyway.

"Moose aren't fans of bright lights. This will be interesting."

"What do you mean, interesting?" Victoria said anxiously, stamping her fashionably covered feet. The three actors positioned themselves at their starting mark on the sidewalk.

"Places! Everyone ready?" hollered Zippo. He talked into his headset. "Background, go! Moose, go." Zippo pointed at Macy, Dylan, and Victoria. "Cue actors. Marker!" A bundled-up crew person scurried in front of the camera, snapped the clapboard, and scuttled out of the frame.

Macy shivered, not only from the chill but also from her apprehension about working with an unpredictable animal. The three of them strolled along, pretending to have a casual conversation. They reached their mark on the alleyway and stopped.

Victoria delivered her line. "Look! A moose!"

The handler stayed off camera, leading the bull moose toward them. The large animal stopped and stared, as if contemplating something. Everyone waited for the moose to continue walking. Instead, he stood still, flicking his ears. Frost heaved out of his never-ending nose as he swung his head around, scoping out his surroundings.

Lights blinked high above them, then flickered out.

"Dammit! Cut!" erupted Zippo. "Two of our floodlights are out. People, our lights froze. Get them back on!"

EVERYBODY LOVES POLAR BEARS

The lighting technician lowered the pole to fix the malfunctioning lights. After tinkering for a few moments, the bulbs turned on, and he hoisted the pole back into position with a hydraulic lift.

"All right, people. Let's do this again. Marker. Everyone, go!" Zippo's voice echoed through the alleyway as everyone hustled into position once more.

Macy hoped this would be the last take because she couldn't feel her toes. Nick had cautioned her to stay warm after her bone-chilling Polar Pond plunge, and in all honesty, she shouldn't be out here. She stamped her feet and wiggled her toes to make sure they weren't frozen.

The three actors moved along the sidewalk, paused, and Victoria delivered her lines. The moose ambled toward them as before.

Everything went as planned—until it didn't.

Without warning, an overhead light came loose and plummeted, clanging along the steel pole until it clattered to the snow-packed alley. It narrowly missed the moose, but the animal jumped back, bellowing with ears flattened.

"That thing better be on a leash!" Victoria cried out in alarm as everyone took a unified step backwards.

The moose eyed them, let out another angry bellow, and charged forward.

"Get behind something! He'll stomp us!" shrieked Macy, zeroing in on the whites of the moose's bulging eyes. She snatched Victoria's hand and sprinted towards a sizeable green dumpster.

The two women wedged themselves behind it, squatting on the packed snow as the handler hollered at the moose and everyone else hollered along with him.

Heart thudding, Macy's breath came fast as she stared at Victoria. "Where's Dylan?"

A blood-curdling scream pierced the night air in answer to her question.

Chapter 30

Macy was stunned into silence as she and Victoria peeked around the dumpster to see Dylan Ford zigzagging out of the alley at warp speed to escape the charging moose. The massive antlers barely missed Dylan's tush as he bolted around the corner of a coffee shop, screaming bloody murder.

"Ooh, poor Dylan!" Macy sucked in air, which promptly stung her lungs.

"I've never seen him haul-ass like that!" Victoria inched up to her feet. "Our action star got a little action tonight. I can't help it; it was funny seeing him flop around and scream like a girl."

"Good thing the handler had the moose on a tether, so he didn't get far. When you see those ears lie back, it's always best to get out of the way." Macy tugged her scarf over her nose and mouth.

The two women waited for the handler to wrangle the moose back to the waiting transport truck, with the animal protection person striding purposefully behind them.

"It's safe to come out now, ladies!" hollered Zippo, waving them forward.

"Good idea. Let's get the heck out of here," groaned Victoria as she grabbed Macy's arm and tugged her toward Zippo's idling van.

Macy spotted Dylan sitting inside the van, looking like he'd fled from murderous aliens in a *Mars Attacks* movie.

Victoria swung open the door. "Well, Mr. Ford, fancy seeing you here," she teased.

"Not funny, Victoria! That moose tried to kill me!" erupted Dylan. "It was terrifying!" He shook like a magnitude ten earthquake. "Get me to my limo and take me to my hotel *now*!" he shouted to anyone who would listen.

Zippo spoke into his headset, and the limo appeared at the curb soon after.

"Oh, you big baby." Victoria chided him like an older sister.

"Come with us. Help me get him settled down," she murmured to Macy. "Our dear Mr. Ford is used to being pampered. If Dylan ain't happy, ain't nobody happy."

"Geez, Victoria, I'm really beat. I was planning on a hot, steamy shower." The last thing Macy wanted was to prolong the evening. What she really wanted was to see Nick and invite him to spend the night at her condo. They'd share laughs at what happened during tonight's shoot.

"Oh, come on. Help me get Dylan to his room, then you can come to mine for a hot toddy before you go home."

"Okay. But I can't stay long." Macy covered a yawn as she climbed into the back seat of the limousine with Victoria and Dylan. "Can the driver give me a ride back to the film office later on to get my car?"

"Of course." Victoria smiled sweetly at the driver. "Randall, would you be a gem and run Bear Woman—I mean Miss Applegate—over to the film office a little later?"

"Not a problem, Miss Miracle," he responded, closing the door.

"Thank God I'm away from that stampeding beast. He could have killed me, you know. But I outran him and narrowly escaped certain death." Dylan's ego kicked in, but he sounded more like a ten-year-old who'd bested a bully.

EVERYBODY LOVES POLAR BEARS

"You sure did." Victoria slipped an arm around his waist to help him out of the limo and into the hotel. She was good at placating her co-star. "But you're fine now. You lived to make another movie."

It amused Macy to see the iconic movie star milking his close call with the moose for Victoria's benefit. Their bizarre relationship baffled Macy. When filming started, they'd bickered, taking constant potshots at each other. Later, Nick joked that Victoria and Dylan messed around between takes, like high schoolers stealing time for a quickie.

Now, Victoria mothered him, and Dylan played right into it. The cast and crew catered to the mercurial Dylan Ford, cranky and narcissistic as he was, because he was everyone's meal ticket to the success of *Everybody Loves Polar Bears*.

Macy took one side and Victoria the other as they guided Dylan onto the elevator, then escorted him to his room. He limped along the carpeted hallway like a war-torn soldier, then swiped his key card over the double doors leading to his suite.

"Where do you want us to put you?" demanded Victoria.

"There," said Dylan, pointing to an elaborate, copper-colored sofa in front of an enormous wall TV with a gas fireplace below it. A long, dark strip of baleen from a humpback graced the wall over the flatscreen TV.

The women eased him down onto the sofa, and he grimaced, which amused Macy. Though the moose hadn't touched him, Dylan acted like he'd been tossed clear across Anchorage and over the Chugach Range.

"Vicky, my love, please do me a favor. Fetch the champagne from the fridge?" whined Dylan, tossing back pills from a prescription bottle.

"Dylan! What did I say about mixing drugs with alcohol?" Victoria responded sternly.

"It's only ibuprofen. Bring the bubbly and come sit with me." Dylan glanced at Macy. "And bring another glass for—"

"Macy," she said politely. "But I don't want any champagne."

"Yes, you do." He looked at Macy with bloodshot eyes. "Tonight was hard on me. I need some cheering up." He patted the spot next to him on the sofa.

Macy had no desire for champagne. Or Dylan Ford. Her only desire was Nick. "I really have to go. I'm exhausted."

Victoria returned with a bottle of the bubbly and set three flutes on the glass coffee table in front of Dylan. "Here you go. I uncorked it for you."

"You're an angel." Dylan took the bottle and filled all three glasses to the brim.

Dylan's phone lit and vibrated on the glass. He ignored it, sipping his champagne.

Victoria picked it up. "It's DeMello." She held it out to him.

He waved it away. "Don't want to talk right now. Let it go to voicemail."

Victoria set the phone back on the table.

Dylan drained his flute in one long gulp. "There. Much better."

Macy left her flute of champagne untouched. She was no longer impressed with Dylan Ford. His tough guy movie persona really was an act. He'd had Macy convinced after watching his action movies.

Victoria rose and wandered around the room, looking for something. "Anyone see my purse?"

"No, did you bring it back with you from the shoot?" asked Macy.

EVERYBODY LOVES POLAR BEARS

Victoria's eyes grew wide. "Oh no! I must have left it in the van after that stupid moose chased us. I must go find it."

"Don't you have people to do that?" asked Macy.

"Not this late at night." Victoria pointed at Dylan. "Don't drink any more booze. You'll pass out!" she barked like a drill sergeant. "I have to go. Macy, wait here. Randall will have me back soon. If not, call an Uber and charge it to DeMello." Victoria vanished out the door.

"Wait, let me come with you!" By the time Macy peeled herself from the sofa and rushed out to the hallway, the elevator doors had closed.

"Dammit!" she muttered and returned to the room.

Dylan's glassy stare, undressing her with his eyes. "Come here and sit down." He patted the spot next to him. Despite his otherwise good looks, he wasn't attractive right now with his highway-map eyes, downing champagne like a barfly.

Macy sat on the opposite end of the sofa with her phone. "I'm calling an Uber."

"Not yet. I've wanted to spend time with you ever since we had dinner." Dylan reached across, snatched her phone, and placed it on the glass coffee table. He picked up her flute and placed it in her hand.

"Drink up," he ordered.

She stared at the flute. "I don't want any."

He scooted next to her and raised her chin. "You are so lovely."

His cell phone vibrated on the coffee table. Then Macy's vibrated.

Dylan ignored his phone, and Macy reached for hers. "I have to get this."

"No, you don't." His hand snaked out and grasped her wrist.

"Let go of me!" She tried to wrench free, but his grip only tightened.

"We're going to have some fun. I have a major pull in Hollywood. I can hook you up." He gave her a hungry look that roiled her stomach. "Just say the word."

"Sorry, not interested!" Inwardly panicking, Macy tried twisting free.

"You know you want me. Every woman does." Dylan's forearm pressed into her chest and forced her back onto the sofa. He laid on top of her and kissed her with such force she could barely breathe. His fingers untucked her blouse, and he slid his hand under it, groping her.

Macy fought to push his hands away, but he overpowered her. She finally freed herself from his disgusting kiss.

"Get off me!" she yelled as he clawed at the elastic waistband of her jeans.

Both cell phones vibrated on the glass. She fought to break free of his grasp when the reality of the situation struck her hard.

I'm being sexually assaulted by the star of Everybody Loves Polar Bears!

The shocking realization made her wriggle and squirm harder, and she screamed. "Let me go! Get off me!"

Dylan was strong, and his body was heavy on hers.

Just as Macy worked a leg loose and prepared to knee his private parts, a door slammed.

"What the hell is going on here?" bellowed Nick, striding into the suite.

Chapter 31

Nick's heart constricted at the sight before him. He couldn't accept what his eyes were telling him.

Dylan Ford is on top of Macy? What the hell! And what is she doing here?

Dylan's head jerked up in surprise. "How did you get in here? DeMello is the only one with a hotel key." Dylan lifted himself off Macy, who tugged her blouse down as she sprung off the sofa.

Nick hurled Dylan's key card at him, and it landed on the plush carpet. "DeMello gave me your key card and sent me to check on you, since you weren't answering your phone. He said a moose attacked you."

Nick's eyes darted from Dylan to Macy in bewilderment. "Macy, what the hell are you doing here?" Anger spiked Nick's tone, and he had a helluva time reining it in.

She pointed at Dylan. "He sexually assaulted me!"

"I did no such thing. She asked me to make love to her. She's been flirting with me during this entire production," Dylan said smoothly in that convincing way that everyone always bought...everyone but Nick.

"Explain why you're here!" Nick glared at Macy, the vein in his temple pulsing as heat surged up his neck.

"Didn't you hear me? Dylan Ford forced himself on me!" she hollered.

"I heard you. But first, I want to know why you're in Dylan's hotel room."

Macy stared at him, stupefied. "Victoria asked me to help her get Dylan to his room. Then she lost her purse and took off and I didn't have a ride back to the film office—"

Nick interrupted. "I would have come to get you," he said, gritting his teeth. "Why didn't you call me?"

"I thought you were busy with filming, or I would have. I was calling Uber when he pushed me onto the sofa and got on top of me..." she trailed off, tears pooling.

"Didn't seem to me you were fighting him off." Nick gaped at Macy in disbelief.

Macy sputtered. "Wasn't it obvious I was trying to push him off me? For crying out loud, Nick, I would never betray your trust!"

"Oh, is that what we have? Trust?" Nick glared at her. "Could have fooled me."

Dylan shifted his lazy gaze to Nick. "So, you two have hooked up. See? I knew she was the production slut. I'll bet everyone has had a piece of her ass."

Nick did it without thinking. His hand curled into a fist and punched Dylan's face.

The movie star stumbled back against the wall, knocking ceramic seals and whales off the shelves. Art pieces flew everywhere and shattered.

"Nick! Stop it!" shrieked Macy. "I only came here because Victoria asked me to help get Dylan settled."

Nick thought Macy seemed like a woman caught doing something wrong. "Victoria is quite capable of handling Dylan." He rubbed his knuckles. Dylan's jaw was harder than he thought.

EVERYBODY LOVES POLAR BEARS

"I'm pressing assault charges," grumbled Dylan as he struggled to his feet. He rubbed his eye. "You'll never work in Hollywood again, Westwood. I'll see to it."

"Go ahead, Dylan," gritted Nick. "Let's see how that works out for you when I share your prior indiscretions with the media." He took a deep breath to calm his ass down.

"Nick, please believe me. I'm not the one at fault here!" pleaded Macy.

"Then you shouldn't have come to his hotel room!" he boomed at her. "Thought you weren't a clone who slept her way to the top." His words dripped bitter acid, and he hated himself for saying it. Dammit, she'd stabbed him in the heart. He wanted to tear Dylan apart.

"Nick, why don't you believe me?" shouted Macy. "This isn't what you think it is! He forced himself on me."

Her words sliced into Nick like a blade. But he knew better than to fall for them. He'd wised up after believing actresses who pretended emotion when all they did was manipulate him.

Never trust actresses. They act their way through real life, just as they do in the movies.

"Nick, you know damn well she's lying." Dylan sounded childish. "She flirts with me every chance she gets. She threw herself at me, wanting me to get her hooked up with the Hollywood elite. You know how these women are."

Disgust crossed Nick's face. "Shut up, Dylan. You're a member of the Celebrity Scum Club with a god complex. You think you're *entitled* to sex, and when it's not offered, you take it. Isn't that what you've done once again here, Dylan? Isn't it? Answer me!" thundered Nick.

"I've done no such thing! No one will believe this woman. No one will believe you either. I'm a fucking icon, worth millions. You can't touch me." Dylan staggered to the bathroom to nurse his swollen cheek and darkening eye.

"Macy, get your coat," Nick said as calmly as he could muster. "I'll drive you back to your car."

"I'll walk, thank you," she muttered. "Apparently, you didn't hear what I said. Or are you choosing to believe your bro, since all you men stick together in these kinds of situations?"

"I know what I saw." Nick swallowed hard; his fists clenched tightly at his sides. He wanted to punch the wall—or the other side of Dylan's pretty face—anything to relieve the anger coursing through his veins. Instead, he drew every ounce of strength to calm down.

"I thought you were different," she said bitterly. "*You're* the clone! And every one of you people are players!" She tugged on her coat, grabbed her purse, and flew out the door, slamming it so hard it shook the walls.

Nick chased after her and stood in the hallway, his foot holding the door so he wouldn't get locked out. "Macy, come back here and I'll drive you. It's too cold to walk!"

"I won't be caught dead with someone who thinks I'm a liar!" Tears streamed down her cheeks as she pounded the elevator button. When the doors opened, she hurried in, and when they closed, her hands covered her face.

"Dammit, I made her cry," Nick muttered, grabbing his cell and tapping the hotel desk phone number. Despite his anger at the situation, he didn't want to behave like the dickhead she used to think he was.

Or still did.

EVERYBODY LOVES POLAR BEARS

"Please get a cab for Macy Applegate," he asked the front desk. "She's on her way down to the lobby, wearing a bright blue parka."

"Yes, sir," responded the voice on the other end.

Nick ended the call and jammed the phone into the back pocket of his jeans.

Geez, Macy, why did you go up to Dylan's room?

Nick went back inside the hotel room to find Dylan sprawled across the bed, dead to the world. He glanced at the empty champagne bottle and Dylan's prescription pills on a table. Par for the course for this loser.

Nick still wanted to punch him into next week, but no point in decking him while he was passed out. He left the room and hurried outside to his SUV. He'd drive over to the film office to make sure Macy got her car started in this hellacious cold and got home alright.

Deep down, he knew Macy had told him the truth, that Dylan had forced himself on her. But he'd been so shocked to find her in Dylan's hotel room, he hadn't known how to respond. Obviously, he'd messed that up big time. Nick wished the freaked-out bull moose would have stomped the narcissistic movie star.

Just the same, he had to tell DeMello. The director would talk to Dylan for the umpteenth time about hitting on the local cast members. *Like it'll do any good,* Nick thought glumly. The only way to put a stop to Dylan's sexual entitlement would be to convince Macy to file charges. At least the dickwad hadn't taken her clothes off, but if Nick hadn't barged in, he most likely would have succeeded.

Nick had some apologizing to do. He wanted to talk to Macy to explain himself.

Why didn't I tell her I believed her?

He was ashamed of himself, but he refused to lose Macy over this. Now she hated him again, and for good reason. He'd have to grovel and dine on crow—apologize for his hot temper. He'd tell her the truth—how the situation had blind-sided him and how sorry he was for not saying he believed her. Nick let out a long sigh and groaned.

What a frigging shit storm.

He pulled into the parking lot in time to see Macy get into her car and fire up her engine. Her tires spun on the icy road as she pulled onto the street and sped off, fishtailing. He thought about following her home to talk to her, then decided it would be best to wait until they'd both calmed down.

He'd get his act together, put his director hat back on, and try not to pummel Dylan the next time he saw him. There was one last scene to film, then that would be it, and he would head back home to California.

And he'd rack his brain for what to say to the woman he couldn't afford to lose.

Chapter 32

Macy spent the next day avoiding Nick. She told no one about the assault, not even Julie—just quietly went in person to the Anchorage Police Department to file a report. She'd explained the situation—including the fact there were only two days left of filming before the production team returned to Los Angeles.

There was never a question in Macy's mind about whether to file a police report, even though Dylan hadn't gotten far with his attempt. Nick had left repeated voice messages and texts, apologizing for the way he'd behaved and encouraged her to report the assault to the APD. He told her it was time Dylan was held accountable for his actions.

At least they agreed on one thing.

Thank goodness Nick showed up when he did. God only knows what would have happened. Macy knew this would be a scandal for the movie, and it would blow up the local and national media if word got out. But she reported it on principle. Let the chips fall where they may.

Dylan Ford's attorney had called her at four a.m. to offer a sizeable financial settlement if she would stay quiet and forget about it. She'd declined, informing him she intended to file a police report in the morning. However, she agreed not to talk to the media until the movie wrapped the day after tomorrow. If this situation halted the production, she'd feel terrible; the rest of the cast and crew shouldn't be penalized for the despicable actions of their box office movie star.

Dylan hadn't contacted her, nor had she expected him to. She was nothing as far as he was concerned, and he'd deny anything had happened until the moose came home. She hadn't appreciated him calling her a slut, especially to Nick.

Since there was one day left of filming, she wouldn't see Dylan Ford again, unless it was in court. And that was fine by her.

Then there was Nick. She had seven calls that she hadn't answered and just as many voice messages and texts. He'd asked Julie to have her call him, but Macy ignored that, too.

"What's going on? Why are you having a lover's quarrel?" Julie had asked before she'd left for the film office this morning.

Ha, lover? Not anymore. Not when he didn't believe me.

She told Julie she didn't want to talk about it. She didn't want to talk about anything regarding last night.

Even though things had gone south with Nick, at least she'd gained film acting experience. And she'd made friends with Victoria, who told Macy she'd put her in touch with her agent.

She'd spent last night staring at her phone, wanting to call Nick. But then she'd recall his remark about her sleeping her way up the ladder and his not believing her, and she'd become angry all over again.

They'd both been too busy on the set to talk, and Macy hadn't seen Nick face to face, anyway. She knew at some point she'd have to confront him. She didn't know when she'd be ready.

If ever.

EVERYBODY LOVES POLAR BEARS

The next morning, DeMello announced they had one last scene to film, where Baby Snowflake gets injured by a male polar bear later in the movie. The cub would be taken from the real Mother Snowflake so the vet could perform surgery.

The location was at a privately owned horse ranch east of town, up on the Anchorage Hillside, nestled in the foothills of the Chugach Mountains. An empty horse barn housed a large cage enclosure the crew had built for Mother Snowflake to simulate a wildlife rescue facility.

The scene required Victoria and Macy to be positioned in front of Mother Snowflake's cage enclosure, showcasing the human-bear relationship Victoria's character had developed with Mother Snowflake and her cub as their protector.

Macy cringed at the movie's message that it was okay for humans to bond with wild animals. In the real world, the same misunderstood theme had gotten people killed in Alaska. But Macy wasn't in charge of this production.

She and Victoria stood on their marks discussing the scene while everyone scurried around them to get everything ready for filming.

Mother Snowflake rested inside her cage, contentedly chewing on a ball of ice the size of a car tire, with frozen fruit inside of it. She was oblivious to the goings on around her.

Nick approached Macy and Victoria in his usual business-like manner. One would never suspect he'd been angry as a hornet after last night's debacle at the Captain Cook Hotel. Macy knew he had a job to do, but she couldn't get over his acting like nothing happened.

Her heart still fluttered at his nearness, but now it was with loathing and a silent, simmering anger. She displayed her resting witch face as he explained how the scene would go.

"Here's what'll happen." He pointed, avoiding Macy's icy stare. "Baby Snowflake is pre-set in the back of the cage."

"Okay," said Victoria. "Then what?"

"When the scene begins, the handler carries Baby Snowflake from the back of the enclosure to the side door, then exits the cage."

Macy watched Mother Snowflake lying relaxed on her stomach, gnawing on her ball of ice. She cringed at the sound of sharp teeth scraping shards of ice, not wanting to know what that would feel like.

Victoria shot a nervous glance at Macy. "What's the cue for my line?"

"When the handler exits the cage and moves to you with Baby Snowflake, you'll interact with him and the cub," said Nick. "Then start your dialogue with Macy. Mother Snowflake will be positioned at the front of the cage, so she'll be behind you for the shot."

Victoria eyed Mother Snowflake, lazily licking her ice ball. "Can't you use the animatronic polar bear for this? You weren't there the night the moose went berserk, and we were all scared shitless. We don't need a polar bear to freak out, too." She turned back to him with a firm stare.

"She won't. Nothing to worry about." Nick shook his head. "The fake bear is only for filming in the water. We can't use it on dry land; it would look bogus. But don't worry. The real bear is inside the cage, so you're safe out here. Keep a safe distance from the cage. You don't want to know what happened to an Australian tourist years ago with Binky, the polar bear at the Alaska Zoo."

EVERYBODY LOVES POLAR BEARS

Macy nodded, recalling the incident.

"What happened?" demanded Victoria.

"She got too close to the cage," said Macy. "Then the polar bear—"

"Stop!" Victoria held up her hand. "I don't want to know, or I'll freak out during this scene."

"Macy, did you get all that?" Nick scrutinized her.

"Yes." Macy's voice dripped with icicles, while avoiding his gaze.

"Did you receive my texts and voice messages?" He offered Macy a tentative smile.

"Yes."

"Did you do what I advised?"

"Yes." She looked away, fidgeting with her hoodie strings.

"We need to talk," he urged.

"I have nothing to say," shrugged Macy with a stony expression.

"We'll talk when filming is done." He stared at her for a moment, then moved off to get everyone ready to film the scene.

"What the heck was that all about?" Victoria gave her an odd look. "So you and Nicky are enemies again? Does this have anything to do with my leaving you at the Captain Cook last night? Sorry about that. I panicked about losing my purse. Had a ton of cash and credit cards in it."

"Did you find it?"

"I left it in Zippo's van, like I thought."

"I took a cab back to my car." Macy debated telling her what happened with Dylan Ford, but knowing Victoria, she'd throttle him into next year and all hell would break loose. Macy bit her lip so she wouldn't say anything.

"Whatever happened between you two couldn't be that bad. Get your heads out of your proverbial asses, kiss and make up," chided Victoria. "I warned you not to break Nicky's ever-lovin' heart."

"He broke mine first." The words popped out before Macy could stop them. She back-pedaled. "I mean, he didn't believe me about something." She waved it off as if it were a trivial matter.

Victoria made a dramatic eye roll. "That's a deal breaker? Honey, if I would have given up on every guy who never believed what I said, I'd be living inside a whiskey bottle on Broken Heart Avenue."

"But you can get any guy you want," said Macy. "You're a glamorous, successful movie star."

Victoria scoffed. "Honey, it ain't all it's cracked up to be. I draw guys to me for all the wrong reasons." She paused. "Nick was the exception. I told you before, no matter how much I flirted and tried to seduce him, he repeatedly informed me we would remain friends. He's the only real male friend I have."

"I've noticed how well you two get along. He seems like he'd be a good friend," Macy said wistfully, glancing at him from across the room.

"Listen to me, Bear Woman," said Victoria firmly. "Don't let this fish get away. Talk to him after we wrap today. Or chances are you won't see him after this."

"I suppose you're right," conceded Macy.

"Then do something about it while you have the chance." Victoria raised her chin to let the makeup person touch up her face while she talked. "I've never seen Nick fall for anyone like he has for you. From where I sit, our Nicky boy is in love with you. Or at least in lust." She waggled her brows at Macy. "Which isn't a bad thing. Like I said, I've tried getting him to go to bed with me for ages."

Macy didn't want to talk about Nick right now, so she conveniently changed the subject. "Have you seen Dylan today?"

"No," said Victoria dismissively. "Since filming wrapped for him yesterday, he took a commercial flight home early this morning. Odd though, he usually stays for the wrap parties."

Macy stared at her as if she'd shifted into an iceberg. "He what? He can't do that! Not after..." She stopped, taking a step back. "He has to stay for—"

"Stay for what?" Victoria's brow furrowed in a puzzled expression. "Why do you care when Dylan goes home?"

Macy hesitated. She didn't want to get into this. Not on the last day of filming.

Nick called out. "Okay, people, we're ready to shoot! Everything is pre-set and we're ready to go." He turned in a circle, talking into his headset and pointing at his crew. "Rolling. Sound! Background... marker!"

The clapboard snapped. Macy and Victoria pretended to have a quiet conversation outside the front of the cage. Each of them wore light gray hoodies and matching baseball caps with *Save Our Polar Bears* embroidered in red.

Nick's voice rang out. "Background, go. Baby Snowflake, action!"

The bear handler appeared, carrying the little bear cub. Another ice ball had been pre-set at the front of the cage, and Mother Snowflake sat on her haunches, pawing at the ice-covered fruit. She leaned forward to scoop up a strawberry with her teeth.

As the handler carried Baby Snowflake to the side door of the cage, the cub suddenly bawled loudly. He continued bawling as the man stepped to Macy and Victoria outside of the cage. The cub squirmed, his paws swiping at the air. Macy leaped backwards to avoid being smacked.

As Macy backed into the steel bars of the cage, Mother Snowflake sprang to action, agitated. She poked her nose between the bars, chuffing and growling. Her paw shot out and caught Macy's hip, yanking her tight against the cage. Her other paw clawed Macy's thick ponytail as the bear tried to pull her between the bars to the inside of the cage.

"Ow!" Macy screamed in panic and agony. Her baseball cap came off as terror seized her.

Mother Snowflake had Macy's thick ponytail in her mouth. The other paw had released her hip, but Macy's skull was being pressed into the bars as the bear tried tugging her inside the cage.

Mother Snowflake tugged so hard it was like a hot knife slicing into her skull. Pain seared through her head like lightning bolts. Her scalp felt as if it was tearing away from her skull with each tug.

Macy screamed, expecting any moment for sharp teeth to pierce her flesh.

Chapter 33

"Nicky! Do something!" screamed Victoria, tugging Macy's arm to get her away from the agitated polar bear. "Mother Snowflake has Bear Woman by the hair!" Victoria's frantic cries were upstaged by Macy's deafening screams.

Macy was so terrified the bear would devour her head, take out an eye, or bite off an ear that she was oblivious to everything else. Mother Snowflake's rancid breath was a putrid furnace blast on her head. Her scalp burned as if the polar bear had set it on fire.

Victoria grabbed Macy's hand. "Bear Woman, listen to me! Nick is distracting Mother Snowflake. When I tell you, yank your head away fast. We'll pull you the rest of the way. Zippo, DeMello, get over here and help!" commanded Victoria.

Zippo and DeMello appeared in Macy's peripheral as they grabbed hold of her legs. Victoria was locked onto something behind Macy, while Macy focused on Victoria's thick false eyelashes. She prayed those spidery things wouldn't be the last thing she'd ever see.

Macy's eyes bulged, tears streaming from the outside corners. Her head had numbed from the intense, throbbing pain in her scalp.

"Hurry Nicky!" Victoria abruptly yelled, "Now, Macy! Pull away!" She grabbed Macy's wrists and yanked her away from the cage.

The bear released her jaws, and the force sent Victoria tumbling backwards. Both women crashed to the concrete floor, with Victoria and Macy sobbing uncontrollably with relief.

"Call nine-one-one!" shouted DeMello. He leaned down and spoke with urgency. "Applegate, are you alright?"

Macy disentangled herself from Victoria and rolled onto her back, rubbing her head. "I don't know. My hip hurts, and my head feels like it's disconnected."

"Westwood! Check her, make sure she's okay. You're the First Aid guy."

Nick appeared over her, his face tight with concern. "She's in shock. Where's the damn ambulance?" He peered intently into her eyes. "Macy, tell me what day it is."

She stared at him, dazed, trying to unscramble her thoughts. "It's...it's uh, Thursday. February something."

"What's my name?" he asked.

"Bruce Wayne," Macy croaked out.

"Oh, no, her brain is really messed up," fretted Victoria.

"No, it isn't." Nick flicked his eyes at Victoria. "Don't ask how I know."

"Oh, God, my head hurts!" groaned Macy, lifting a hand to her forehead.

"Lie still while I check you for injuries." Nick palpated his hands up and down each arm and each leg. "No broken bones. Let's examine your head." His fingers delicately explored her scalp, and she winced. "Contusions, but no bleeding. The bear didn't bite you. Can you stand?"

"I think so, but my hip hurts. I think it hit a bar or something." Macy blinked back tears of relief, hanging onto Nick's calm voice. She couldn't control her trembling.

EVERYBODY LOVES POLAR BEARS

Nick slid his arm around her waist and lifted her to her feet. She wobbled, and he steadied her. She crumbled into him and sobbed on his shoulder.

"Oh God, Nick. I was so scared. I thought I was going to die."

"But you didn't." He held her tight against him. "Don't worry, you're safe with me. I've got you," he soothed, rubbing her back. He barked out an order. "Someone, get her a chair!"

A canvas camp chair appeared, and Nick eased her onto it. "Ambulance is on the way. Rest here until they come."

The room quieted as cast and crew surrounded her. Macy expected a clapboard to snap and someone to yell, "Rolling! Action!"

She glanced up to see a triumphant Mother Snowflake sitting innocently on her haunches, as if nothing was amiss, with Macy's baseball cap dangling triumphantly from her mouth... *Save Our Polar Bears* prominently displayed above the bill.

Phones went up all over the room, pointing at Mother Snowflake with her prize, as the first responder sirens grew closer.

Tears flowed as Macy clung to Nick, seated next to her, stroking her hand. She was thankful to be alive.

And thankful Nick and Victoria had acted quickly to save her.

Chapter 34

Nick wanted to apologize for everything that had happened, but he didn't know where to start. Humor had worked with Macy before, so he figured he'd try it again. Anything to take her mind off the pain.

"Is there any chance for make-up sex?" he asked, trying to get Macy to crack a smile. He kneeled next to her sofa on the floor of her condo, where she rested on her back.

Macy blinked. "That's a heck of a thing to say after I nearly had my head ripped off by a polar bear. I wouldn't have a head right now if it weren't for you. I'd be slightly dead."

Nick had stayed by her side since the incident that afternoon. He was grateful she hadn't been seriously hurt or, worse yet, killed. It could easily have gone that way.

"The doctor said to keep these bags of frozen peas on your head to reduce swelling," Nick said as he gently positioned a bag between a pillow and the top of Macy's head.

"Ow!" she recoiled from the pain as Nick wrung out a warm washcloth and sponged her forehead.

"I've not had make-up sex. Maybe when my head stops feeling like a walnut in a nutcracker. Do I even have any hair left or do I look like Gollum?" She reached up to feel.

"Snowflake yanked out a healthy portion, but she left enough to make a bird's nest back here." He fingered her strands. "It's full of stinky bear saliva. When you feel up to it, I'll help you wash your hair."

She rested her hand on his arm. "Tell me again what you did while I was busy praying that I wouldn't die."

Nick's pulse ticked up as he recalled the horrific scene. "I broke into pieces when I saw that damn bear trying to pull you into her cage. Bears aren't physicists. They don't understand why humans don't fit between the bars. I distracted her, so she'd let go of you." His stomach twisted, recalling his desperation to reach Macy before it was too late.

She stared up at him. "How did you do that?"

"I went inside her cage." Nick relived his terror upon entering the cage unarmed. He'd always carried a weapon for aggressive wildlife when he'd hiked and fished on the Kenai Peninsula—but never on a movie set.

Macy's eyes grew enormous as he unfolded the story.

"I grabbed one of the frozen bowls with ice and fruit and snuck over to Mother Snowflake—didn't realize how huge she was until I got close. As a child, I'd watch zookeepers bang bowls of frozen fruit on the ground to loosen the ice. The polar bears took that as a dinner bell. So, I banged that bowl of ice on the floor, praying it would be enough to distract Snowflake."

Macy shook her head. "I didn't know any of that was going on."

"You didn't hear me banging that effing bowl?"

"I only heard a grunting, growling bear and a shit ton of screaming. Including my own," said Macy. "Then what happened?"

"I slid the ice ball across the floor to Mother Snowflake. When she turned her attention to it, Victoria and the others pulled you away from the cage while I bolted out of it."

Macy reached up to cup his cheek. "Thanks for helping me, Nick. Now I owe you for saving me twice and botching two polar bear scenes." He thought he saw forgiveness in her eyes and hoped she was no longer mad at him.

"I'm not keeping score." He lifted the washcloth and dipped it into a bowl of warm water. "I'm sorry you had another scary incident. DeMello is afraid you'll sue."

"I didn't sue the first time, and I won't this time. Geez, this isn't L.A." Macy let out a sigh. "You warned me to keep my distance from the cage, and I didn't. So, it was my fault."

"DeMello plans to compensate you for your medical costs, and for pain and suffering, same as he did when you fell into Polar Pond. Since you aren't in the actor's union, he said he'd take care of everything. He has more than enough funds to cover it."

She gave him a doleful look. "Your movie people must think I'm the klutz of the century after messing up two of your scenes."

Nick laughed. "Well, there's talk that you'd be perfect in a sitcom."

"Will we have to film today's scene again?" she asked.

"Nope. We have enough. When you feel up to it, DeMello will fly you down to Los Angeles to film your dialogue with Victoria in front of a green screen. We'll edit in Mother Snowflake behind you." He pressed a fresh package of frozen peas against Macy's scalp.

"Wow, DeMello will do that?" She grasped his wrist and squeezed it. "Thanks so much for helping me, Nick. This is getting to be a habit."

"You're welcome. It was a bit of a situation."

They shared an awkward silence. Then both talked at once and laughed.

EVERYBODY LOVES POLAR BEARS

"You go first," he said.

"I was so angry with you. We left things in a mess the other night," she intoned.

"Yes, we did. Partly my fault," he responded.

"Partly?" She gave him a questioning look.

"Well, you shouldn't have gone to Dylan's room to begin with." While it bothered him to no end, he was trying to let it go.

"I know." She heaved out a sigh with a forearm across her forehead. "Okay, partly my fault. But there's still the minor detail of you not believing he'd sexually assaulted me."

"I know, and I deeply apologize for that. It's just... when I saw him on top of you, all I saw was red. Nothing either of you said sunk in after that."

"But when you didn't believe me, that really hurt, Nick. After everything we've shared while working on this movie, I thought you would've had my back." She shot him a wounded glance.

"I did have your back when Dylan called you a slut," he pointed out.

She transferred her gaze to him. "Yes, thank you for that."

"Despite my anger, I couldn't stand by and let him insult you." He'd rather erase his memory of decking Dylan, but the satisfaction it brought him made him feel good. He would do it again in a heartbeat.

"Victoria said he flew back to L.A. early this morning. The cops won't like that. He'll have to turn around and fly back to Anchorage because I'm not dropping the charges."

"Nor should you," said Nick. "I admire you for having the courage to report it."

"I loved what you said to him about seeing sex as an entitlement," said Macy. "I have to admit, when you said that, I had a hard time staying mad at you."

"I'm sorry I lost my shit. Can you please forgive me? It's just that I considered you my girlfriend, for lack of a better word. We never discussed exclusivity, so I guess I assumed it."

"Do you believe me now?" she said quietly.

"That's why I called and texted you to file a report with the APD."

"Thanks for that. Your messages helped with my decision." Her eyes watered. "I forgive you Nick, if you forgive me." A tear slipped down her cheek.

"It's a deal." He kissed away her tear.

"Oh, yeah. Dylan's attorney offered me hush money to stay quiet about it."

"What did you say?"

"I said I didn't want it. But I agreed not to say anything until after the movie wrapped, which was today." She shrugged, letting it hang there.

"Plan to tell the media?"

"I won't have to. When the cops inform Dylan he must return to Alaska to face the sexual assault charge, it'll be all over the news. Then every woman he ever did this to will come forward, hopefully." She thought for a minute. "By the way, did Dylan tell the cops you decked him?"

"Not after his lawyer said you planned to file a police report. He called me early this morning before he flew out, asking me to talk you out of it. I told him, sure thing. He thanked me and took off."

EVERYBODY LOVES POLAR BEARS

"So, you lied to him. Because I don't remember you talking me out of it."

He smiled. "Guess it slipped my mind." Nick's expression became solemn. "I'm proud of you, Applegate. You have integrity. I like your style."

"So...tell me about make-up sex."

He raised his brows. "If I give you a play-by-play, it'll ruin the real thing."

"All right then, I'll wait for the real thing." Her smile widened, warming his battered heart. "I'm sorry, Nick. It was a dumb decision to go to Dylan's room."

"And I'm sorry about my sleeping-your-way-to-the-top comment. I didn't mean it. Like I said, all I saw was red."

"Come here." She reached up to grasp his shirt collar and tugged him close. "Give us a kiss."

He thought she'd never ask. He kissed her tenderly, so as not to cause her added discomfort. Her pain medication had helped ease her soreness, but he didn't want to make anything worse.

When he finished kissing her, he figured they'd said enough about the Dylan incident. They needed to move on.

Nick brightened. "When you feel better, I'll tell you about my new production company."

She sucked in a breath. "Your what?"

He nodded, smiling. "I've been thinking about it for quite a while. Chatted with DeMello when he asked how long you and I had been—as he put it—kibbitzing. We had a pleasant chat."

She laughed. "Kibbitzing? Tell me more. I want to hear."

"I've been thinking of hanging out my shingle as an independent filmmaker. I'd like to make a positive difference in the film industry, and starting my own production company is the best way to do that."

"Wow, Nick. That is amazing. Good for you, figuring out what you want." She steadied her gaze on his. "I guess everyone knows about us now, huh?"

"You could say that. Everyone is rooting for us, though. You know, movie romance and all." He offered a contrite smile. "I'm not only here to nurse you back to health, but to offer you a formal apology for what happened on set....and to ask you if you'll be my official date for the wrap party."

"Oh, gosh. I've lost track of time. When is it?"

"Tomorrow, on Valentine's Day. Dinner at five and then a party afterward on the Quarter Deck at the Captain Cook Hotel." Nick wanted to make things right between them before he had to fly back to L.A.

"That sounds fun." She held a hand to her head. "I hope my head feels better by then. I'll hit Julie up for something to wear. A nineteen eighties cocktail dress, maybe, from the wardrobe department."

"Wear that same pink dress you did for the wedding scene in the movie when I kissed you for the first time. You look hot in that thing. See if Julie will let you keep it." He'd thought of a million ways to get her out of that dress when he first saw it on her.

"What else did DeMello say when you chatted?"

Nick lit up, recalling his conversation. "He saw how much happier I was, being back in Alaska. He said he'd figured it out after a while, but to his credit, he said nothing until I brought it up."

"He seems like an okay guy. You two seem to hit it off."

"We've worked on several productions together." A wide-open smile spread across his face. "DeMello says Alaska has an opening for a state film coordinator. They're planning more projects here." He paused. "He also told me you're exactly what I need."

"And what is that?" she whispered, tugging at his heart.

"A woman who knows her own mind and knows what she wants. He also said we should work on getting along for over five minutes at a time. So, what do you say? Be my date tomorrow at our final wrap party?" He waited expectantly.

"Only if you'll be my Valentine, Bruce Wayne. Come here and give us another kiss."

"You don't have to call me that anymore since the jig is up. I'm back to being Viktor Andreanoff." He leaned down to kiss her.

"Will you stay with me tonight? I don't want to be alone. I want you to hold me and keep frozen peas on my head."

"I'll start now. Move over." Miraculously, they both fit on her sofa. It did Nick's body good to stay quiet and still with her.

Who would have thought coming home to Alaska would be the best decision he ever made?

Chapter 35

Macy sat next to Nick at the director's table as DeMello stood front and center in the large Quarter Deck ballroom on the tenth floor of the Captain Cook Hotel.

"Here's a toast to our picture wrap: to the best cast and crew in Anchorage, Alaska! And a colossal thank you to our on-screen talent. All of this was just words on a page until each of you brought *Everybody Loves Polar Bears* to life. Excellent job, everyone!" He raised his glass, and everyone clinked glasses at their tables.

DeMello continued. "When I wrap a movie, I have a longstanding tradition of giving out a congeniality award. I reward those who pour their heart and soul into our productions, collaborating with every member of the team."

"The congeniality award for *Everybody Loves Polar Bears* goes to...drumroll please...Miss Macy Applegate for her positive attitude, especially in the face of danger when things went south. Come up here, Macy!"

Shouts erupted, and everyone clapped. A rush of warmth swept over Macy and her heart swelled when DeMello motioned for her to come forward. With heated cheeks, she rose from her chair and moved to the front of the room to cheers and applause.

"You've set a good example for the rest of us," said DeMello. "Your good nature, positivity, and get-it-done attitude helped make this a fun film. People enjoyed working with you. And believe me, that's not always the case with some actors." He raised his brows and smirked.

Macy figured he referred to a certain movie star who'd skipped town. The audience tittered as snickers worked their way through the room.

DeMello held up his hand. "Thank you for being such a good sport after your unexpected ice plunge into Polar Pond and Mother Snowflake, wanting you to be her roommate."

"Or her afternoon snack!" shouted Zippo to scattered laughter.

"One scary incident was enough, but two..." He shook his head. "I'm so sorry this happened to you. You should produce your own Alaskan reality show about the dangers of polar bear conservation," he joked, offering her a framed certificate. "The cast and crew signed this."

"Thank you," said Macy graciously. "But I think there are enough reality shows about Alaska."

"Never too many! But film them in the summer," shouted Zippo, raising his glass.

Everyone laughed, nodding in agreement.

Macy studied the signatures. Directly under her name was Nick Westwood's elaborate signature. She glanced at him, and he gave her a thumbs-up.

"Oh, and one other thing," said DeMello, producing a smaller frame. "The production team thought you should have this." He gave her a five-by-seven photo of Mother Snowflake sitting in her cage with Macy's baseball cap in her mouth.

"Check this out." Macy held up the photo for everyone to see.

"Snowflake's trophy!" someone yelled, and everyone laughed.

"This was my first time working on a movie." She glanced around the room and caught Victoria's eye. "Saying goodbye to friends is the hardest part. I'm amazed at how any film production comes together with all the things that can go wrong. It was a privilege working with all of you incredibly talented people who make the magic happen. I'll always treasure this experience." Her gaze caught Nick's warm one. "Thank you for allowing me this opportunity."

Macy took her seat to whistles and applause. She passed the photo around their table.

"Nick Westwood, come up here," said DeMello, giving him the eye.

The man Macy had grown to love casually sauntered up to his boss.

"Westwood is the Captain America of this production," said Zippo, to more whistles and cheers.

Warm fuzzies rolled around Macy's chest, watching Nick's colleagues shower him with accolades.

DeMello held up a framed eight-by-ten photo of Nick, with a giant bowl of ice raised over his head, like a crazed wild man. "This is in honor of you saving the day twice so your Valentine could be with us here tonight. First you pulled her out of Polar Pond, then you risked your life with Mother Snowflake."

He motioned to Macy with a wink. "You must like her or something."

The room broke out in laughter as Nick smiled. "Or something," he said, glancing in her direction.

"Not only that, but you also by some miracle...and I don't mean Victoria...got Dylan Ford to mush a dogsled team!"

The room once again exploded into laughter and applause.

"Hey Nicky! Enlighten us with what an oosik is!" shouted Victoria.

EVERYBODY LOVES POLAR BEARS

"You're really going to make me do that?" He blushed, and Macy thought that was cute.

"Well, yes, my dear. One of our extras asked if I wanted to see his oosik, remember?" persisted Victoria, despite the outburst of snickering and laughter around the room.

She stood, with a hand shading her eyes, glancing around. "Skippy? Are you here?"

"Right here!" an older man's voice called out. Skippy stood up from one of the extras tables.

Macy thought he looked spiffy in his oversized wool suit jacket with a flannel shirt and a bolo tie.

Victoria spread her arms. "Well, one of you better explain it!"

Judging by the uproarious laughter, Macy figured most in the room knew what an oosik was, but she loved how Nick seemed bemused by the way he covered his mouth and shook his head.

"I'll take care of that for you, Mr. Westwood," said Skippy, standing sober and proud. "Lemme put it this way for our California friends. When a walrus gets a hard-on, you might say he stays hard no matter what."

"Thanks for that scientific explanation, Skippy," hollered Victoria. "Special effects, turn me into a female walrus!" Unabashed, she raised her glass to scales of laughter.

Zippo stood and quieted the room. "No one knows this, so I'll fill you in. After Nick got Macy out of Polar Pond on that film shoot and helped her until the ambulance came—" Zippo cleared his throat. "Nick brought Skippy on board, who was homeless. He hired him on the condition he'd come to work sober. And Skippy did just that each time he reported to work. Way to go, Nick." Zippo applauded, and everyone else did, too.

Skippy raised his hand. "I want to thank Mr. Westwood for giving me a chance and hiring me at a low point in my life. With your help, I got off the street and had a reason to sober up," said Skippy. "And I have you to thank for it."

Nick dipped a nod at him. "You're very welcome. I'm happy it worked out. Thanks for working with us."

"Good on you, Westwood!" someone called out, and the room erupted in applause.

Macy sat, dumbfounded. She didn't know Nick had done that. He'd not mentioned it. Of course, he wouldn't. He just quietly did it on his own. Thinking back, she'd noticed Nick talking to Skippy sometimes between takes, but she'd figured he was being friendly, as he was to everyone on the set.

DeMello stepped up to the front. "Okay, everyone! Enjoy your dinner, and Happy Valentine's Day!" He took his seat to cheers and applause.

Nick gave Macy a peck on the cheek. He leaned across her to toss an offhanded comment at DeMello. "I can kiss her now, since we've wrapped."

DeMello raised his glass. "Westwood, feel free to do whatever you want with her now. And have fun doing it!"

Macy regarded the man of her dreams, loving how hot he was in his suit without a tie, the top of his shirt unbuttoned. She admired his unassuming attitude. Not cocky....not at all arrogant. She scolded herself for thinking those things about him in the beginning.

Nick had turned out to be the opposite of what she'd first thought. Not only that, he was also one hundred percent Alaskan through and through. That thought alone made her girl parts skitter.

EVERYBODY LOVES POLAR BEARS

She had an overwhelming desire to be alone with him. Her head was still tender even though her headache was gone, but that didn't prevent her from desiring intimacy with Nick. She'd not experienced make-up sex, but from the way everyone raved about it, she couldn't wait to get started. The mere thought of Nick liquidated her every sensation, which was the exact opposite of their first encounter. She chuckled at how she'd detested him in the beginning.

When the band played a Nat King Cole classic, "L-O-V-E," Nick danced with her under a thousand points of silver light cast by a disco ball.

When the song ended, Macy took Nick's hand and led him to the elevator, kissing him all the way down to the sixth floor.

Chapter 36

Macy closed the door to the room Nick had reserved on the sixth floor of the Captain Cook Hotel. Nothing fancy, just a room with a bed, because that's all they wanted. He'd reserved the room for two nights so they could stay in bed the entire time if they chose. They could each use some rest, along with all the other things she had in mind.

For most of the evening, she'd levitated up onto a subarctic cloud, cruising moonbeams while she danced with Nick, especially after the lights on the dance floor had dimmed into shades of blue, sprinkled with cobalt stars, thanks to the light-design crew. They'd topped it off with undulating northern lights along the ceiling for a mystical, magical effect.

Nick stood watching the clear, wintry skies above Anchorage through the immense window. Faint glimmers of green and lavender toyed with the top of the Chugach Mountains as Macy came up behind him and slid her arm around his waist.

"Are you happy to be home again?"

"I'm happy to be here with you," he said, tugging her against him. "My home isn't Anchorage, though. It's down on the Kenai Peninsula."

"I know. I meant happy to be home in Alaska. Why didn't you tell me about Skippy?" she asked. "That was a generous thing you did."

EVERYBODY LOVES POLAR BEARS

Nick shrugged. "You know how hard it is for homeless folks in the winter here. I just wanted to help him out. He reminded me of my dad."

"I admire you for doing that." She produced a small box. "Happy Valentine's Day, Nikolai." With hands folded tightly, she backed up and watched with eager anticipation as he opened it.

Nick gave her a what-did-you-do look and pulled the ribbon, which came off easily. He took his time unwrapping the gift, just to tantalize her. When he finally opened the small box, he broke out in a smile. He lifted a miniature dip net with a red ribbon tied in a bow on the tiny handle.

Macy fidgeted. "Keep going. There's more."

Nick took out a blue candy heart and read it. "You've won my heart." His eyes met hers. "Yours was a hard one to win."

"Read the other one."

Nick picked up the second heart and offered it to her. "You read this one."

She suddenly felt shy. "I know what it says."

"I want to hear you say it," he said softly, nudging her to take it.

She fought to control her emotions. "Love you forever," she said, staring at the piece of candy, unable to control the tremor in her voice.

Nick's smile had a spark of eroticism as he kissed her, long and deep. When he drew back, he carefully placed everything back in the box, closed it, and set it on the table. "Where did you find that tiny dip net?" he asked incredulously.

"From a tourist shop on Fourth Avenue." She slid her arms around his neck. "Wanted you to have a reminder of the first time we were naked together."

"Ohh...I don't need a reminder. That's one thing no guy could ever forget."

"It was sad watching the crew pack everything up and load it onto the semi-truck trailers. Gave me an empty feeling," she said.

"I know what you mean. I'm always bummed when a movie wraps," admitted Nick. "It's like separating from a family."

"I'll miss Victoria. And Zippo and DeMello. And...you." Her voice tremored.

"Hey," he said, stroking her cheek. "DeMello is flying you down soon, and you can stay with me. I plan to keep my home in L.A., even when I'm working in Alaska on film projects."

She swallowed. "Really?"

"Once you're in the lower forty-eight, you'll take Hollywood by storm."

She snorted. "Not sure I want to. I've been doing some thinking after you talked about your own production company." She gazed up at him, squeezing his hands. "I don't want the Hollywood glitz and glamour anymore. Maybe you could hire me as a narrator for your documentaries about saving narwhals or sea lions? I'd love to narrate one about a moose-dropping festival."

"You mean where they drop moose from an airborne C-17?" joked Nick.

She rolled her eyes. "Right. Everyone knows droppings are moose turds."

He lit up. "I love your idea. You would narrate for my documentary?"

"Hey, I have a fabulous narrative voice. I could be the female version of Morgan Freeman. I'll even audition for you." She crossed her arms and tilted her head. "But only on one condition."

"What's that?"

"That you let me finish my flipping reading."

"I think we can skip that at this point." Nick moved close and kissed her.

She drew back, breathless. "And you can stay at my condo as long as you like. Julie is heading to L.A. to work on more films. DeMello liked her work on this movie and offered her more gigs."

"Then I'll cover Julie's part of the rent when I stay there," he said.

"I own the condo, so you'll have to pay me."

"Can I work it off by being your man toy?" He lifted her chin. "I say it's time we get down to business. I want to give you *my* Valentine."

She offered him a seductive look. "Let me guess..."

He undressed her ceremoniously, taking his time. When at last she stood naked before him, she meticulously returned the favor. They stood in the center of the room, drinking each other in until Nick led her to the bed and eased her down on the satiny comforter.

"Tell me something." She stared up at him. "What did you wish for that night at the Foraker Roadhouse when we watched the northern lights?"

He stared right back, his eyes brimming with passion. "I wished for you to love me."

"What a coincidence. We had the same wish, and both came true!"

He leaned down for a gentle kiss, then lifted off, gazing down at her.

"I can't wait to work with you on your new projects." Macy brushed the hair back from his forehead. "Let's make Alaskan wildlife documentaries. But not about polar bears—not for a while, anyway." It thrilled her to have something to look forward to now that filming had ended.

Nick chuckled as he moved over her, kissing her shoulders. "Maybe we'll do something about whales. After all, everybody loves whales."

He blazed a trail of fire with his kisses that had her writhing under him. "I love you, Applegate. Happy Valentine's Day," he breathed as she let him take her.

"Oh God, I love make-up sex!" she hollered happily as she reached her summit on Denali.

When Nick released, he uttered such a loud moan that Macy was sure every polar bear on every ice floe in the Arctic Ocean was sure to hear it.

Because as everyone knows...everybody loves polar bears.

Thanks so much for reading Everybody Loves Polar Bears! If you enjoyed reading it, I'd be thrilled if you'd tell your friends and family about it...and please take a moment to post a rating or review online at your favorite retailer. Reviews make an enormous difference for my success as a writer, and they help readers discover the story.
You can read Cupid's Kerfuffle, a free book in the Polar Paired Series by signing up for my newsletter at https://dl.bookfunnel.com/q9nsmlcw6v
If you enjoyed this story, check out my other romantic comedies!

EVERYBODY LOVES POLAR BEARS

ALSO BY LOLO PAIGE
Standalone books in The Wandering Hearts series from The Wild Rose Press!

When Riley Sullivan takes a cruise, she unlocks an adventure with Killian, the charming front singer from the popular singing group, Irish Thunder—who spice up their shows by taking everything off but their kilts! Sometimes, the only way to find love is to dream it into existence.

Travel writer Dayna Benning tours Europe to write a feature story for a travel magazine. When she accidentally meets Alex Mendes, she senses a chemistry with the silver fox airline pilot. But unless she can mend her fragmented heart, Alex will forever remain a fantasy.

LOLO PAIGE

Want more hot romantic reads? Check out LoLo's Firefighter Romance Series!

New York Times bestselling authors have this to say about the Blazing Hearts Wildfire series:

The strong women and smoking hot men who fight wildland fire, written by a lady who knows from personal experience. These are fiery page-turning reads. —Kat Martin, New York Times bestselling author

Cinematically plotted in a spectacular, dangerous setting...smoldering passion where fire isn't the only heat! —Cherry Adair, New York Times bestselling author

Read on for an excerpt from Hello Spain, Goodbye Heart!

Chapter One

Dayna Benning eyed the ominous Portuguese sky hovering over the roiling sea. Glancing left across the expanse of empty beach, she raised a hand to shade her eyes. She squinted at two beefy guys next to a just-as-beefy Jeep with water rescue equipment. Beach lifeguards. One pointed binoculars at her.

Ahead of Dayna and intent on her mission, Mariko Waller ignored the lifeguards and strode toward the surf, clutching a small, plastic bag with its gray, gritty contents. Wind made a mainsail of her unzipped jacket and her bare feet scrunched sand as she tramped toward thundering surf, like a Viking warrior on a sea quest.

"Don't toss him on the sand, get him in the ocean!" Dayna called out to her best friend.

She zipped up her jacket and plunged bare toes into the warm, white sand, loving how it massaged every crevice and felt oh-so-good after walking around Nazaré all morning. The air had turned chilly, but the sand warmed her toes, like a soothing pedicure.

As Dayna straggled after Mariko, she eyed a yellow sign with two fluttering red flags: *Praia fechada surf perigoso*. Didn't take rocket science to figure it warned of dangerous surf conditions.

We shouldn't be out here.

Dayna quickened her pace with one eye on the brawny guys who had climbed in their Jeep and were now speeding toward them, no doubt to kick them off the beach.

"Hurry! Go-go-go!" yelled Dayna, the crashing waves eating her words. She spun around to see if anyone else might interrupt their mission. A tall man strode toward them from the boardwalk.

Oh great, probably a cop or something.

"Come on, Mariko, get Harv into the ocean!" ordered Dayna. The lifeguards and the dude coming up from behind were gaining on them.

Mariko broke into a spasmodic run, opening her bag and holding it high.

Dayna sprinted, her Girls bouncing hard as she clutched an open gallon bag of meticulously preserved rose petals. "Hurry, my boobs are trying to kill me!"

The sound of a shrill whistle competed with the roaring sea as Mariko's legs spun like an Olympic sprinter. Dayna chuckled at seeing her friend run. Mariko detested exercise.

As the fast-approaching vehicle closed in on them, one lifeguard stood in the passenger side, pumping his whistle.

"Do it now!" Dayna barely heard herself against the pounding waves.

Mariko shook the bag as if shaking dice in a million-dollar bet on a craps table. "He's being stubborn—I can't get him out!"

"Oh, for crying out loud." Dayna snatched the bag and hurled the contents onto an emerald wave that curled and broke at the shoreline. "Come on, Harv, swim!"

The women watched with bated breath as the ocean swept his ashes away from the shore. "Goodbye, Harv," said Mariko, her hand in her heart.

EVERYBODY LOVES POLAR BEARS

Dayna slid an arm around Mariko's waist in a sideways hug, then pulled her arm away to dig into her bag of petals.

"Rest in peace, Brother." She flung a fistful of petals after Harv's ashes, but a powerful wind gust blew them back at her.

"What's this?" spluttered a deep voice, followed by spitting and coughing.

Dayna turned to behold the lofty guy who'd followed them out to the roaring surf. He swiped at the rose petals sticking to the stubble on his face. She jerked around like a chicken, then froze after showering this person with dead rose petals.

Dayna's hands flew to her mouth. "Oh, I'm so sorry! I mean *lo siento*."

The Jeep slid to a stop in the sand and a lifeguard jumped out, motioning them toward the boardwalk, traffic cop style. "*Saia da praia,* please leave the beach."

Mariko held up her strong, slim fingers. "Please sir, we were just leaving."

The lifeguards waited until all three dutifully headed toward the boardwalk before driving away.

Dayna shot a sideways glance at the gentleman with his salt-and-pepper hair, blue and white rose petals stuck to him like magnets.

"*Lo siento, lo siento,*" ventured Dayna, as she stepped through the white sand.

"I speak English," he said, picking a petal from his sleeve. "And it's *desculpa* in Portuguese."

An American. A rather *hot* American.

"Right...*desculpa*." Dayna's cheeks heated. She berated herself for not studying her Portuguese language program before leaving California. Writing deadlines devoured her time up to the minute she'd boarded the plane. She'd clicked 'Submit' on her phone while scooting down the jetway, relieved she'd made her last deadline.

Hot American plucked another rose petal stuck to his fleece jacket. "What flowers are these? Do you want these petals back?" He held out his fist as the three of them moved toward away from the beach.

"Yes, but wait until we get out of this squall." Dayna's hair glommed to her face. "They are, or rather were, Blue Dragon roses. Harv grew them, and he started me growing them in my garden back home."

"Beautiful flowers. My auntie grows these." He strode briskly between Dayna and Mariko.

"They're my favorite," gushed Dayna, thrilled that this gentleman appreciated the pride and joy of her garden.

"At least we got Harvey into the sea, just like he wanted." Mariko glanced at Dayna as they stepped up onto the wood boardwalk.

Dayna squeezed her friend's arm. "Yes. That was important."

Hot Guy pointed his sunglasses in Mariko's direction. "And Harv was...?"

Dayna motioned to her friend. "Mariko's husband. We had to scatter his ashes before the lifeguards chased us off. Honestly, I didn't know you were so close behind us. Sorry, the petals blew into your face." The wind fluttered the sleeves of her gray and orange *San Francisco Giants* jacket.

His hair blew into a sexy, wild man vibe. "Blame it on this blustery weather." He turned to Mariko. "I'm Alex. So sorry for your loss." Sympathy crossed his face, despite the sunglasses hiding his eyes. Dayna suspected those peepers would be in happy agreement with the rest of his fine features.

EVERYBODY LOVES POLAR BEARS

"Pleased to meet you, Alex." Mariko tilted her head, dipping her chin. "I'm Mariko and this is Dayna." She retrieved her flip-flops from her small tote bag.

When Alex smiled at Dayna, the sun came out for her, despite the real one hiding behind purple storm clouds.

"Mariko, I'm sorry you didn't have time to say words for Harv." Dayna wished the lifeguards hadn't chased them away so fast. "I had my eulogy on the ready."

"We'll do it next time," said Mariko. "I'll light candles for him in the cathedrals on our tour."

"You're a good woman." Dayna admired Mariko's ability to conceal her grief, as if reserving it for her very own. Dayna couldn't hide her pain. Instead, she wore it like a sandwich board. All the money she'd spent on counseling after her divorce—what a waste.

The wind re-styled Mariko's short black hair. "Let's get out of this breezy weather. Besides, I've worked up an appetite. Alex, the least we can do for dousing you with dead roses is to buy you lunch."

Dayna noticed Mariko eyeballing him like she wanted *him* for lunch. Not if Dayna could help it. He'd appeared on *her* menu first.

"Yes, it's the least we can do," echoed Dayna. "We have a bus to catch, so it'll be a quickie."

"I have time for a quickie." He grinned at the two women.

"We only have forty-five minutes." Mariko tapped her wristwatch as if this beach would combust if she didn't eat.

This guy could easily fit the mold for the article she'd written for Society Magazine, *The World's Ten Sexiest Men*.

Alex unzipped his jacket and more petals fell out. He bent and scooped them up before the wind seized them and tucked them into his pocket.

Dayna sat on a nearby bench to strap on her sandals. Brushing sand from her toes, she squinted up at him. "So, what do Blue Dragon rose petals taste like? Sorry about that. Would it help to say *desculpa* again?"

Alex laughed. "Unnecessary. Here, I'll help you up." He offered his left hand, and she zeroed in on it.

Gold glinted his finger. Married.

Damn.

Get Hello Spain, Goodbye Heart!

ABOUT THE AUTHOR

LoLo Paige is an award-winning author who writes romantic comedy and romantic suspense. She's been honored with several awards, including an RWA award for her romantic comedy, *Hello Spain, Goodbye Heart*. Her books about wildland firefighting have achieved critical acclaim and commercial success, topping Amazon Bestseller Lists in the U.S., Canada, and Australia, and *Publishers Weekly* has featured her books. As a former wildland firefighter, LoLo's true story about escaping a runaway wildfire won a 2016 Alaska Press Club award.

Follow me on Amazon! https://www.amazon.com/stores/LoLo-Paige/author/B0872KT8QS *Want to learn more about my books? Sign up for my newsletter on my website!*

[LoLo's Website](https://www.lolopaige.com)
[Facebook](https://www.facebook.com/LoLoPaigewildlandfire)
[Instagram](https://www.instagram.com/lolopaige/)
[Goodreads](https://www.goodreads.com/author/show/20305632.LoLoPaige)
[BookBub](https://www.bookbub.com/authors/lolo-paige)

---

1. https://www.lolopaige.com
2. https://www.facebook.com/LoLoPaigewildlandfire
3. https://www.instagram.com/lolopaige/
4. https://www.goodreads.com/author/show/20305632.LoLoPaige
5. https://www.bookbub.com/authors/lolo-paige

Don't miss out!

Visit the website below and you can sign up to receive emails whenever LoLo Paige publishes a new book. There's no charge and no obligation.

https://books2read.com/r/B-A-MQPK-DPGSC

BOOKS 2 READ

Connecting independent readers to independent writers.

Made in the USA
Middletown, DE
17 September 2024